A
SHORT
GUIDE
TO

GROUPS

GROUPS

THE ART OF LEADING
COMMUNITY

JARED MUSGROVE
& JUSTIN ELAFROS

PUBLISHING
BRENTWOOD, TENNESSEE

978-1-0877-8079-5

Published by B&H Publishing Group
Brentwood, Tennessee

Decimal Classification: 302.3
Subject Heading: GROUPS \ CHURCH GROUP
WORK \ INTERPERSONAL RELATIONS

Cover design and illustration by Matt Lehman.

1 2 3 4 5 6 • 27 26 25 24 23

Dedication

*To Christy, my wife and faithful partner in pursuing
Jesus together. To Cooper, Beckham, and Addie, whom
I love with all my heart. Thank you for all the
ways you challenge and love deeply.*
—Justin

*To the men of Beta Upsilon Chi (BYX, Brothers Under
Christ). God used this lifelong brotherhood born of smaller
groups to shape me into a greater husband, father, and leader
through community. And I'm not the only one.*
—Jared

Acknowledgments

WE BOTH SHARE IN these pages the fruit of years of dreaming and leading alongside fellow groups ministers and spiritual friends.

Thank you, *Groups Team Classic*: **Kristen Ainsworth**, **Travis Cunningham**, **Mike Dsane**, **Jason Holleman**, **Maury Hundley**, **Tyler Powell**, **Marc Ritthaler**, and **Tori Salinas**. Leading and loving the people of God alongside each of you shaped us into the men and pastors we are today.

We also want to thank **Mary Wiley**, publisher extraordinaire. You believed in this project from day one. Your enthusiasm, energy, and edits helped us stick the landing. We love working with you! You share fully in the fruit born of this book.

Thank you, **J.J. Seid**, our partner and friend at Community Leadership Collective. For nearly a half decade you have taught us a thing or two about community and leading community; whether it was coleading CLC or sitting around the fire in fellowship, you continue to encourage us and there is much of you in these pages.

Thank you **Bill Willits**, the groups sage in our lives. So many insights, laughs, shared love of all things British, and great wisdom for the long haul in leading community ministry. Thank you for your friendship!

And thank you **Matt Chandler**, for always supporting, praying, and empowering us to lead with our gifts. You are a personal encourager to us both; and a champion for authentic community transformation in the local church. Keep leading boldly as the Lord leads you.

Authors' Note

THIS IS A BOOK about community written *in* community with one another. We wouldn't dream of attempting it any other way.

And in this spirit we designed the book for you to read and discuss in *your* community. It's for group leaders as well as vocational ministry staff in a wide array of churches and parachurch ministries.

Almost all of us have some type of small group discipleship environment.

And you might love it.

You might be frustrated with it.

Or maybe you have lost hope entirely regarding small groups.

This is a book for all of us.

This is a book for people who love the possibilities of small groups. And for those who want to.

Contents

SECTION 1

Why Groups?

CHAPTER 1

Why Groups?

THIS IS A STORY we will never forget. A few years ago, Naomi, who is a widow, was invited to her daughter's small group. She did not believe in Jesus and was forthright and polite about that, but she was at group every week for months. As they grew closer together, she was included in the community. She still did not attend the church services or profess belief in Jesus. One night as the group was having honest conversation with one another, they asked her why she kept coming to group, not being a Christian or a church attender. Some of them admitted that she was more devoted to the group than *they* were. Her answer: "I keep coming here because nobody in my life ever loved me like you have."

Groups are not easy ministry, but such ministry bears the kind of fruit in the above story. Maybe you are a group leader on the edge of giving up. We've been there too. Maybe you are launching groups for the first time ever, and you're dealing with an excess of nervous energy and excitement. We've been there many times as well. You're either a person who loves groups or a person who *wants* to love groups. Either way, this book is for you.

Groups are an ancient art form that demands the attention of church leaders and members today. They are an invitation into all that God has for us, and part of that inheritance is one another.

Groups are an art, not a science.

A lot of approaches to groups are formulaic: that + this = a great group. But neither a person nor a group of people can be reduced to an equation. That's the truth of Naomi's story. It was supernatural relational care that kept her coming back to the group. The love she found in a small group eventually led to her attending a church service for the first time in her life, which eventually led to her calling Jesus her Lord and Savior. That's why groups matter. There was no formula for Naomi's transformation. It was simply a group of true Christians in community, ready to receive and love her.

The success of groups isn't a formula; it's relationships. *There is no lasting transformation in a person without another person.* To facilitate such transformation, we have to create an interdependent relational system in our churches. This takes time, intentionality, and a lot of prayer.

Groups are certainly art, but what is good art? There are a few agreed-upon rules and standards, and even those go out the window many times, and we are often amazed at the impact when they do. Similarly, groups are unpredictable, which drives some of us crazy. There are so many variables and unknowns.

Yet the unknown is right where we need to be. This is the place where our faith is tried and refined, where heaven meets earth. Uncertain circumstances and unfinished people are most often the focus of God's greatest transforming work. It's here that God moves in the life of groups.

WHO HAS GOD GIVEN YOU TO LOVE?

Good art challenges us. It may make us change our mind or transform our thoughts, and it may make us uncomfortable. The right goal for groups is to be good art. Nothing is more uncomfortable than walking into a room of people you may or may not know, aware that they are going to ask you about the Bible you haven't opened in weeks and the sin that plagues your heart. Groups are uncomfortable because you can't hide or just show up—at least not if it's a good group. You have to participate.

Groups also challenge us like a good movie or book. We look at groups like we look at good art, desiring one thing: a transformative experience. But the way we find that transformative experience seems counterintuitive.

Groups rub up against our preferences like an art piece in shocking colors that just don't seem to work. Yet groups also speak to our inherent human desire for change, betterment, encounter, and transformation. Each of us has to choose to commit to the intense (and often awkward) interpersonal friction necessary for transformation. It is easier to say, "I changed my mind" or "I'm now different" because I read a book, took a class, had a coaching call, listened to a podcast, or went to a conference. All those are good things and can be *parts* of the picture of transformation and growth. Indeed, *there is no lasting transformation in a person without another person.*

The people in your group are a partial inheritance from the Lord right now.

So, whom has God given to you? Where has He placed your church? What's unique about your church? Context? Who's coming? And do you *love* them? *The people in your group are a partial inheritance from the Lord right now.* This is why we lead and launch groups. We seek to obey God's imperative command to love one another. The New Testament records more than fifty individual "one another" commands. As you read them, ask yourself how many of these we can fully accomplish in a typical Sunday morning worship gathering? How about in a small group setting?

The One Anothers of the New Testament (CSB)

1. "Be at peace with one another" (Mark 9:50).
2. "Wash one another's feet" (John 13:14).
3. "Love one another" (John 13:34).
4. "Love one another" (John 13:35).
5. "Love one another" (John 15:12).
6. "Love one another" (John 15:17).
7. "Love one another deeply as brothers and sisters" (Rom. 12:10).
8. "Take the lead in honoring one another" (Rom. 12:10).
9. "Live in harmony with one another" (Rom. 12:16).
10. "Love one another" (Rom. 13:8).
11. "No longer judge one another" (Rom. 14:13).
12. "Welcome one another, just as Christ also welcomed you" (Rom. 15:7).
13. "Instruct one another" (Rom. 15:14).
14. "Greet one another with a holy kiss" (Rom. 16:16).
15. "When you come together to eat, welcome one another" (1 Cor. 11:33).

16. "Have the same concern for each other" (1 Cor. 12:25).

17. "Greet one another with a holy kiss" (1 Cor. 16:20).

18. "Greet one another with a holy kiss" (2 Cor. 13:12).

19. "Serve one another through love" (Gal. 5:13).

20. "If you bite and devour one another, . . . you will be consumed by one another" (Gal. 5:15).

21. "Let us not become conceited, provoking one another, envying one another" (Gal. 5:26).

22. "Carry one another's burdens" (Gal. 6:2).

23. "With all humility and gentleness, with patience, bearing with one another in love" (Eph. 4:2).

24. "Be kind and compassionate to one another" (Eph. 4:32).

25. "Forgiving one another" (Eph. 4:32).

26. "Speaking to one another in psalms, hymns, and spiritual songs" (Eph. 5:19).

27. "Submitting to one another in the fear of Christ" (Eph. 5:21).

28. "In humility consider others as more important than yourselves" (Phil. 2:3).
29. "Do not lie to one another" (Col. 3:9).
30. "Bearing with one another" (Col. 3:13).
31. "Forgiving one another if anyone has a grievance against another" (Col. 3:13).
32. "Teaching . . . one another" (Col. 3:16).
33. "Admonishing one another" (Col. 3:16).
34. "Overflow with love for one another" (1 Thess. 3:12).
35. "Love one another" (1 Thess. 4:9).
36. "Encourage one another" (1 Thess. 4:18).
37. "Encourage one another" (1 Thess. 5:11).
38. "Build each other up" (1 Thess. 5:11).
39. "Encourage each other daily"(Heb. 3:13).
40. "Consider one another in order to provoke love and good works" (Heb. 10:24).
41. "Encouraging each another" (Heb. 10:25).
42. "Don't criticize one another" (James 4:11).
43. "Do not complain about one another" (James 5:9).
44. "Confess your sins to one another" (James 5:16).
45. "Pray for one another" (James 5:16).

46. "Love one another, and be compassionate and humble" (1 Pet. 3:8).
47. "Maintain constant love for one another, since love covers a multitude of sins" (1 Pet. 4:8).
48. "Be hospitable to one another without complaining" (1 Pet. 4:9).
49. "Just as each one has received a gift, use it to serve others" (1 Pet. 4:10).
50. "Clothe yourselves with humility toward one another" (1 Pet. 5:5).
51. "Greet one another with a kiss of love." (1 Pet. 5:14).
52. "Love one another" (1 John 3:11).
53. "Love one another" (1 John 3:23).
54. "Love one another" (1 John 4:7).
55. "Love one another" (1 John 4:11).
56. "Love one another" (1 John 4:12).
57. "Love one another" (2 John 5:1).

In the hundreds of times we've walked congregations and leaders through this quick exercise, we've never heard anyone say most or all could be achieved on a Sunday morning. Groups are the right place for these "one anothers" to come to life in our congregations.

GROUPS IN SCRIPTURE

In our limited views it's easy for us to think group ministry came about in the last forty years, but groups are not a new idea. They have been gathering for multiple millennia. God set apart the Israelites so they would be a picture to the nations of what it looks like to follow after God. Even in exile, where they didn't have much cultural favor, God tells them to

> build houses and settle down; plant gardens and eat what they produce. Marry and have sons and daughters; find wives for your sons and give your daughters in marriage, so that they too may have sons and daughters. Increase in number there; do not decrease. Also, seek the peace and prosperity of the city to which I have carried you into exile. Pray to the LORD for it, because if it prospers, you too will prosper. (Jer. 29:5–7 NIV)

Settling into a particular place with a particular people was God's vision for community and blessing to the world. We carry on the charge God gives to Abraham: "I will bless you and make your name great, *so that* you will be a blessing" (Gen. 12:2, emphasis added).

Jesus continues this idea with the twelve disciples in John 13:34–35: "A new commandment I give to you, that you love one another: just as I have loved you, you also are to love one another. *By this* all people will know you are my disciples, if you have love for one another" (emphasis added).

Jesus shows we don't come together just for the sake of ourselves but also for the sake of those who do not yet know Christ. We gather to love one another, and by that love others see God's Son.

In John 17, as Jesus prays to the Father, He is also looking through history and praying for you and for me. He says, "I do not ask for these only, but also *for those who will believe in me* through their word, that they may all be one, just as you, Father, are in me, and I in you, that they also may be in us, *so that* the world may believe that you have sent me" (John 17:20–21, emphasis added).

"By this," "so that" the world may believe the Father sent the Son. The Scriptures don't reveal a people of God who only focus on *one another* or only focus on *neighbor*. To truly follow Jesus is to do both.

As you show love for one another, "they will know you are my disciples." There is a missional aspect to the family of God as we love one another. Francis Shaeffer says it this way, "Love—and the unity it attests to—is the mark Christ gave Christians to wear before the world. Only with this mark may the world know that Christians are indeed Christians and that Jesus was sent by the Father."[1] It's a unique, Christian love.

It's hard for many of us to get outside of our "knowledge transference" mindset even when we want to. It's easier to talk at people than take the time to build the relationships such love and unity require. The call of Christian community is not to download information into one another; it's a call to live relationally in deep, unified community. *The less relational your church is, the less transformational your church will be.*

The less relational your church is, the less transformational your church will be.

Many of us in the West don't have a value of community, especially compared to "collectivist cultures" in other parts of the world where community is of utmost importance. No, we increasingly value personal space and individuality, often above all else. Yet the Scriptures speak of the people of God as the opposite. The church tends to create a lot of opportunities to *do*, but we have few places to *be*. The deepest level of community should be found in a spiritual family, and in most churches that is clearest in the group ministry.

When Jesus says to His disciples, "They will know you by your love," He wasn't just speaking to award-winning small group members. He was saying this to Matthew the tax collector and Simon the Zealot, two men who, viewed from our time, were political enemies. A quick history lesson teaches us that Matthew would have been hated by his fellow Jewish brothers and sisters and seen as a traitor to his people because he carried forth the taxation of Rome on the Jews. Further, as with most tax collectors, Matthew would add a higher tax rate than Rome was asking for in order to take a larger cut for himself. He would have been disowned by his family and community, but Jesus invited this man into his small group. This was no small amount of human risk. On the other side of the relational equation is Simon. Simon saw the oppression of Rome as a judgment from God and believed it was his responsibility to bring about redemption for the Jewish people through the destruction of Rome. This usually meant resorting to physical aggression, murder, or assassination. Yet again, he was brought near by Jesus.

To these two Israelite group members, Jesus says, "Love one another." Can you imagine?! There would not have been two enemies who hated each other more.

To a much lesser extent than this extreme example, groups need to be a space where the "least of these" and the "churchgoer" can not only sit next to each other but also be in fellowship with each other. Many groups' philosophies or habits have the tendency to exclude one or the other, but Jesus calls us to be together regardless of class, station, income level, or political persuasion.

This is the call of Christ: to love one another. Love that leads us to fulfill the great commandment and the Great Commission. The church has been meeting for thousands of years, and it's our turn to step in and faithfully steward one another toward unity and mission through love.

GROUPS AND THE PRIESTHOOD OF BELIEVERS

> But those who want to be Christians in earnest and who profess the gospel with hand and mouth should sign their names and meet alone in a house somewhere to pray, to read, to baptize, to receive the sacrament, and to do other Christian works. . . . Here one could set up a brief and neat order for baptism and the sacrament and center everything on the Word, prayer, and love. —Martin Luther[2]

If you had asked Martin Luther what it would take to be a true community of faith in a local church, he would have told you that it takes the priesthood of *all* believers. That is, all believers can read and understand Scripture's plain meaning, have equal access to communion with God, and are actively involved in the work of ministry. Said differently, there's no special class of mediators for knowledge of God, presence of Christ, or ministry to others.

This is a doctrine he fought for years to reclaim in the Reformation, so he was certainly invested.

Then, if you asked Martin Luther (so kind of him to entertain all our questions) how the priesthood can be activated in a local church, his answer would revolve around small groups meeting in homes. He'd go on about how meeting in homes leads to deeper expression of some spiritual realities surrounding the priesthood of all believers, and these groups are best positioned to "do other Christian works" that are not possible in the institutional church meeting once a week. Joel Comiskey writes, "Luther saw the potential of the house church and had a vision of meeting in homes for deeper expression of faith, which was absent in the institutional church. We know from Luther's writings that he could see great possibilities for ministry in the small house churches, but he refused to go that route because of cultural ramifications."[3]

Martin Luther thought small groups in homes were the way to activate the priesthood of all believers, but he never started them due to fear that it might create a lack of control. Before we pile on Martin, though, we should recognize that he was facing the same frustration that we often do: a lack of trust in God to make other brothers and sisters who Scripture calls them to be.

"Sounds Good in Theory"

One church leader recently shared with a group, "Yeah, priesthood of all believers sounds good in theory," then pantomimed a verbal ellipsis with a shoulder shrug meant to imply that it doesn't really work in practice. It doesn't pan out. Hire staff to do the work. If you can pay them, you can fire them. Volunteers are messy—like farming. So mechanize the ministry.

Yes, all of this can be said with a shrug. We understand this line of thinking. We get it, but it's also what keeps so many of our churches from seeing an empowered priesthood. Our first mistake may be that we too often talk about the "priesthood of the believer" (singular) instead of the biblical "priesthood of all believers" (plural). It's not about individuals; the community of saints is the primary consideration when it comes to church.

The biggest opposition we see to the activation of the priesthood of all believers in our church and yours is that favorite idol of church leaders: control and comfort. These two are so intertwined that it is nearly impossible to unravel them. The inner critic of the church leader who's lived too many disappointments throws his soul's hand in the air and gives in to the voice that says, "What you can control can't hurt you." Far too often we listen to that voice instead of God's.

We are so committed to arranging a happy little church that suits *our* needs and comforts and caters to our gifts, but God often thwarts those efforts by allowing for our continued frustration. You feel it, right? That's the loss of wonder. It happens because we want a perfectly controlled church but also want to make an impact for God's kingdom. That dichotomy can't hold. It has devastating consequences when we try to carry it out.

Luther experienced deep depression in realizing that he couldn't bring himself to release this kingdom of priests as he knew was best. For some it may be a lack of joy in equipping saints. You may be unable to stand the saints altogether. You grow short with them. You find ways to avoid them. You figure it'd be easier to run a company, a capital campaign, or a Christian nonprofit. Honestly, it might be.

Equipping the saints for the work of the ministry in a local church is like agriculture. If you're called to pastor and lead in the church, you're running a farm, not a manufacturing plant. Live human beings and their souls are your sheep and soil. And there's no chance of seeing lasting growth without an activated priesthood in your church. People are our true capital campaign. Flesh-and-blood human beings are our building program. The priesthood of *all* believers (plural) is both our occupation and our product.

People are our true capital campaign.
Flesh-and-blood human beings
are our building program.

Relationships of Trust Are Stronger than Theory

The good news is that this priesthood already exists. It only has to be discovered, developed, and deployed throughout your church. And it all comes down to trust. While there's no pain like broken trust in vocational ministry, there's also no fruitfulness like when trusted saints serve as God's priests.

First Peter 2:9 speaks to the sleeping giant of frontline ministers that exists right now in church small groups: "You are a chosen race, a royal priesthood, a holy nation, a people for his own possession, that you may proclaim the excellencies of him who called you out of darkness into his marvelous light."

Every time a small group meets, the potential for harvest exists. People want to be changed and to see those they love change. Church leaders often can't spread themselves far enough to sustain interpersonal connections throughout their church, but many hands make light work when the priesthood of all believers is equipped and entrusted to serve by loving one another. This has always been the best means of true growth and transformation in a local church. That's the power in the local priesthood of believers meeting in small groups throughout the week. Martin Luther envisioned it. He didn't activate it, but we can. The beginning and end of this activation are trust and love.

Developing a Love for One Another in the Church

The call is clear: we are to love one another, revealing the heart of Christ to a watching world. It's about relationships. *The less relational your church is, the less transformational your church will be.*

But how? The "one another" commands we discussed earlier cannot be practiced in a single hour in a worship service. So many of these commands involve our direct, physical ministry to one another and to our neighbors. It happens best in proximity. There are dozens of opportunities for disunity whether it's due to isolation because of working from home; a tense (isn't that putting it mildly?) election year; the wildly differing considerations, convictions, and information regarding public health; parenting styles; or worship song preferences. At every turn we can seek to love one another well, not being blown off course by the frustrations of even one of these matters, let alone all at once, as the world expects.

For the church, this isn't the fire drill of the day. This is the continued movement of God through one another in your small group.

Groups exist for community with God and one another. Small groups are the greatest opportunity a church has to consistently practice the "one another" commands of Scripture. Now more than ever, we need groups to lead the pursuit of true biblical friendship and practice the "one another" commands, using all our gifts to share the gospel together. We need the "one anothers" to guard and guide our relationships.

Groups exist for community
with God and one another.

Our greatest fear is that we have created churches that have no room for these commands. We don't create environments where members of the body use their gifts "for building up the body of Christ" (Eph. 4:12), and too many of our ministry environments create space for one to three people to use their gifts (mostly emphasizing teaching) to build up the body. In doing so, we limit our churches.

What if we didn't? That's the art and opportunity of groups ministry. It can change a church. We've seen the two are inextricably connected. They are one. In fact, we go so far as to say:

> *So goes groups, so goes the church.*
>
> *So goes the church, so goes groups.*

So, where do we start? The "one anothers" are not a sequential game board. They are a palette of possibilities and creative obedience. Just like groups, the "one another" commands are *an art, not a science.* Like the Israelites in the wilderness or Jesus leading His disciples, this art begins with people.

A practical start is to pray the "one another" passages listed earlier over your group. When you are together or apart, you can tangibly ask the Lord to make these commands an increased reality of your shared ministry and multiplication. They're both your game plan and your prayer list.

The "one anothers" are God's guide to healthy relationships with fellow brothers and sisters. Write them out and keep them with you. Make cards and pray one a day as a group. Take time every group meeting to specifically pray one or two or more of them over the group.

With repetition comes practice, connectedness, and growth. These commands were necessary for the original recipients, and they are commands for us today, so we can ask for help obeying them. Together.

In the following chapters we highlight some aspects of groups ministry. This isn't a strategy book, but we will share some real practicalities. This isn't a philosophy book, but we've got some things to make you think. This isn't a poetry book, but we will attempt to be artful in some places. There's variety. You can skip around. You can read straight through. You can have it on your desk or coffee table for a jolt of inspiration. This is a book for people who love groups ministry. Or want to.

We will repeat some key phrases on purpose. We want them to stick with you and be a guide as you read and seek to implement the learnings in this book:

> *There is no lasting transformation in a person without another person.*

> *The less relational your church is, the less transformational your church will be.*

> *The people in your group are a partial inheritance from the Lord right now.*

> *Groups exist for community with God and one another.*

> *Groups are an art, not a science.*

> *So goes groups, so goes the church.*

> *So goes the church, so goes groups.*

We want to introduce groups to you all over again: the most widespread, diversified, exciting, and essential ministry a church can engage!

Discuss

1. What has been your most memorable experience as a group member?

2. If you've led a group before, what experience brings back the most joyful memories? The most painful?

3. At this moment in time, what is the biggest challenge you face in leading a group?

4. What is the biggest need you have right now to help you be a more effective group leader?

5. How many of the "one anothers" does your church address during a Sunday gathering? How might groups facilitate more of the "one anothers" being lived out in the body?

6. How can you lead your group in practical ways to implement the "one anothers"?

Groups Transform

CHAPTER 2

Home Base for Transformation

LIST THE TOP FIVE sermons that most impacted your life.

Could you name them?

Now list the top five people.

Which is easier?

We've never done this little exercise with a group that didn't say the people came to mind immediately. The sermons, well . . . not as quickly. God uses sermons to fortify the body of Christ each week. They are like meals this way. Sustenance. However, true change often comes when God uses others to sharpen, convict, or challenge us. Full transformation in a person takes another person, and that's the possibility of what God will do in and through you in the lives of His people in community. When we think back on our own lives and how we both have changed and been transformed by God through the years, the people in our life marked us most. That's God's design for the church as His agent of transformation in people's lives.

So goes groups, so goes the church. So goes the church, so goes groups.

As we speak with other group leaders from around the country, many struggle to identify what a group *is*, especially in connection with other ministries. Groups—whether study, community, or missionally based—are the most adaptable environment you may have at your church, so defining them clearly is far more challenging than defining the kids ministry or college ministry philosophy and strategy. Mostly because it's serving such a wide range of people. Defining expectations is equally challenging. You may find that many hope groups are the one-stop shop for missions, teaching, care, and marriage ministry in the church. That's not a sustainable model.

So goes groups, so goes the church.
So goes the church, so goes groups.

Groups exist to know God and experience His presence through a spiritual family. They provide an opportunity for intimacy, mutual support, equipping, love, and sharing what the Lord is doing. The Scriptures speak of the people of God primarily through the lens of family[1] or the body,[2] individuals in light of the whole. These images call to mind a place of belonging.

However, we know that we are fighting back against something deep within us: Western individualism. We don't have a value of community. Instead, we have a high value of individualism. Sure, we know we "need" others but not really, right? We only want to participate if it fits into our perfectly structured calendar. This is why groups are hard. Groups will (and *need* to) change how we live because we are committing ourselves to a group of people. Many of us enter into relationships with a consumer mindset: What am *I* going to get out of this? What if there is someone/something "better" out there? But we can't have community without commitment, and we can't have a mission without commitment, either.

In their book *Slow Church*, Christopher Smith and John Pattison highlight how the speed of our culture is quickening (high-speed Internet, rapid rewards, fast food, and so forth). As a result, many in the church have been formed to want church and discipleship with minimal effort and maximum speed. Joseph Hellerman adds, "Spiritual formation occurs primarily in the context of community . . . long term interpersonal relationships are the crucible of genuine progress in the Christian life . . . people who stay, grow. People who leave, do not grow . . . it is a simple but profound biblical reality that we both grow and thrive together or we do not grow much at all."[3]

It's good and right to treat work with speed, efficiency, and excellence. But, when we apply that style directly onto our relationships, it's destructive. In our overly digital, fast world, most are both more connected than ever before and more lonely. Relationships are chances to slow down, marinate, and be. Fast relationships tend to become boxes to check off as opposed to life-giving sustenance. Yet we are both hurt and healed in community. It's where God does His best work. *Groups exist for community with God and one another.*

Groups serve as the nervous system of the body of Christ. A group serves as a home base. They are the vehicle for community as members weave in and out of other discipleship environments in their church and life, providing a fertile ground for discipleship to go deeper and help foster longer lasting fruit.

Many churches have wonderful outreach training that incorporates in-class instruction and field experience to help members grow in their understanding and experience of how to share the gospel. Often, instead of signing up for this class alone and meeting new people you may never see again after the class is over, we encourage groups to sign up together. Groups develop deeper relationships and a strong missional rhythm together as they connect God's mission with their everyday purpose.

It may be that your group doesn't want to participate in a particular class together, and that is again why groups need to be the most adaptable environment at your church. Everyone won't always attend the same discipleship opportunity, so, in this scenario, your group time should become a time of processing and sharing together what the Lord is teaching you separately. Some group members may be in a women's Bible study, while others are in outreach training, and still another is meeting with a pastor or counselor to better their marriage. In seasons like these, the greatest need is not another study to go through together. People need a time of processing and sharing what the Lord is teaching them in that particular season. Group time is the perfect time to download what God is doing in each member to the benefit of all members. Not all transformation is linear, and not all transformation happens in a learning environment, but all transformation is relational.

TRANSFORMATION AND LEARNING THEORY

Adults still have a lot to learn. It's just not about facts and figures and Bible verse references at this point in our lives. Knowing your Bible isn't just naming all the threes, sevens, tens, and twelves; it's "Do you *live* the book?" And for that we need one another to be transformed into the image of Jesus.

There is no lasting transformation in a person without another person. Or persons.

While this concept has received some attention recently (more on that later), it is first (and best) supported by the way of Jesus. He moved from the crowds, to the Twelve, to the call to action. True transformation in men and women has three major movements: **a new idea encountered**, **transformational moments in community**, and **living the transformation**.

There are so many opportunities for this transformational path to take shape in an intergenerational small group. At the forefront such a group looks a lot more like the body of Christ with varied ages, stages, backgrounds, ethnicities, and ranges of walks with God. Nothing is more beautiful than the body of Christ gathered in a living room. Together. For the gospel. For however long the Lord has you together, never let your inter-generational group members lose the wonder of Christian unity across the ranges of our lives and experiences with Him. True transformation and disciple-making happen as those ahead help those farther behind along the path of following Jesus, and we are sharpened most by those who are not like us.

Transformation in childhood is so different from what we as adults of all ages experience. Adult transformation comes not just from a new idea or knowledge but from a life lived, an encounter with another believer, and living by truth. As a leader, you must know your Bible, but don't forget to also *live* your Bible in the company of spiritual friends.

There are three core elements we can learn, pray over, and work toward in our multigenerational groups. These elements correspond with our Christian faith, the Bible's story, and how adults truly change: a transformational idea encountered, transformational moments in community, and living the transformation.

A Transformational Idea Encountered (John 3:18; Rom. 12:1; Phil. 4:8)

As Jesus walked among people, He often taught in stories or parables that challenged norms and opened up new ideas. The modern equivalent of this moment might be a group member sharing about a sermon that was meaningful to them or the confession of sin by a group member that signals to another that there is a way that seems right to man but in the end leads to destruction. Maybe a group member shares about a population in your city who needs help, and you were unaware of that need until that moment. New ideas can initiate transformation and, often, action.

Encountering new ideas moves our minds to identify a solution to the problem. Freedom or emancipation is the main theme of this beginning transformation by the renewing of the adult mind, regardless of age (Rom. 12:1–2). Freedom from sin is freedom to obey Christ and to live as transformed people. This is where the Philippians 4:8 command to think on "whatever is true, . . . honorable, . . . just, . . . pure, . . . lovely, . . . commendable . . . [excellent]" begins.

Within the new idea encountered is also where the gospel begins to take root. It's in embracing the freedom-giving gospel that you "know" your old self was crucified; you believe if you've died with Him, then you will also live with Him; you know that death no longer has dominion over Him (Rom. 6:6–11, 14–23). New ideas explored over time often bring deeper understanding and commitment. You know that you know. You are strengthened in your inner being so that Christ may dwell in your heart through faith (Eph. 3:16).

But it cannot end there. No adult thinks or transforms alone.

Transformational Moments in Community (Eph. 4:1)

Jesus spent most of His time among some combination of the twelve disciples. Honest, probing questions were asked and answered forthrightly, and they wrestled with Jesus's teaching. Similarly, small groups allow for verbal processing and wrestling through Scripture or life events in a safe environment where admonishments occur based in personal love and concern for God's design. The small group is where knowledge of God, self, and friends begins to form and transform the persons in the group.

This small group space is critical to how adults of any age conform more to the image of Christ. When you have a multi-generational group, recognize that we are all learning, forming, and transforming along this path. The community is key. The people in your group, regardless of age, are relational creatures. Ephesians 4–6 helps us see that *there is no significant transformation in a person apart from another person.* Each man or woman in a small group is in danger of being tossed to and fro, but when we speak the truth to one another in love, we grow up in every way into Him who is the head, Christ. We can't walk with Him alone. We are designed to need one another as a core.

This walking together is the ministry of presence. It's listening, sharpening, and loving one another while being gathered together. It's the core of our being transformed. And it is what groups can be best at providing.

When we sit with others, truly sit with them, we are bringing our body in alignment with our relational state so that we can receive in accordance with the truth. This "relational mind" is what allows the truth to impact the depth of our heart. Have you ever had the experience of being in a difficult situation and someone you don't know well shares a Scripture reference with you? We have. Most of the time it's annoying. But later that night, as we sit around the fire with good friends and unpack a difficult situation, that same Scripture ministers to the soul as they share. Why? We are in the "relational mind." We feel deeply with the other person and are open to what they have to say, even though it's the same passage our acquaintances shared earlier.

While transformation often happens gathered around the fire or in the living room, our faith must also be lived.

Living the Transformation (James 1:19–25; 2:14, 26)

With transformation in your walk with God, there is always a call to action. Action is our right response, our worship, for all God has done. This is the journey outward. You take the transformation done with a small group into your home, your work, and your community. This is the step of the path where you are not a hearer who forgets but a doer who acts, blessed in your action (James 1:25). Transformation is visible in your outward life.

Upon the ascension of Jesus, He sends His disciples to the crowds and the nations, accompanied by His Spirit but not by His physical body. As we carry this same message and accompanied by this same Spirit as we are called to do in the Great Commission (Matt. 28:19–20), God's work in our life is clearly on display. Just as the disciples went out to serve two by two, we are called to serve together. It may be serving shut-ins in a local nursing home or blessing first-year teachers at your local schools.

It may be street evangelism at local shops or prayer walking your neighborhoods. It is your journey outward, together. It must occur because we know that faith—and community—without works is dead.

So, regardless of the age range in your group, there's work to do together. We are all on a pathway to further transform and become more like Christ today than we were yesterday. That's the constant commonality in an intergenerational group. There's always opportunity for growth in the gospel. It never gets old, and there's never an end to our ability to learn.

LEARNING THEORY

As we consider groups as home base, we must also consider established learning theory[4] and how it impacts how we cultivate community spaces.

Passive Teaching Methods Retention Percentages

- Lecture (5%)
- Reading (10%)
- Audio/Visual (20%)
- Demonstration (30%)

Participatory Teaching Methods Retention
Percentages

- Discussion Group (50%)
- Practice by Doing (75%)
- Teach Others (90%)

As humans we are awful at learning but really good at imitating. In fact, in the data above we see we retain 90 percent of what we teach to others. Group becomes the space where members can teach one another what they are learning.

Statistics say you will retain roughly 10 percent of what you're reading right now (or hear on a Sunday morning sermon or in a classroom environment), but you will retain 90 percent of what you teach to others.

By practicing what is taught on a Sunday morning, we retain roughly 75 percent. So, if our pastor preaches on fasting and then we fast that week (putting into practice what was preached), our retention level increases. This same concept is true across any number of topics that need to move from our head to our hands.

Building opportunities for groups to read, hear, practice, and teach will yield the strongest recall and, ultimately, disciples who are learning and growing.

CREATING ENVIRONMENTS AND PATHWAYS

In our experience many churches have teaching environments that last anywhere from four weeks to nine months. While knowing the time frame can help determine what to study simply by identifying how many sessions of learning may be involved, we also must consider that there are real, dynamic people in the room who have needs and even distractions. The biggest goal is not to determine what to study but to create an environment that encourages relationships that far outlast the group. Much of spiritual formation is slow, deliberate, from "one degree of glory to another" (2 Cor. 3:18), so deep relationships and extended time are necessary.

Relational, transformational opportunities don't just develop out of thin air. Although groups ministry may sometimes seem somewhat effortless (especially if it's going well), it takes significant effort and prayer to rightly order discipleship pathways for our people. Following Jesus isn't a plug-and-play church program. It isn't linear and cannot be reduced to a particular learning environment or time. When we try to force it into this mold, we unintentionally force that which is dynamic to that which is static. However, following Jesus is dynamic! "In him we live and move and have our being" (Acts 17:28). He gives spiritual gifts to His body so that we can grow and partner with Him in the ministry He has laid out before us. If I (Justin) had the gift of mercy (I don't often) or the gift of administration (ask anyone . . . I don't), then what does it look like for me to use that gift for the building up of the body? How does that play into my following of Jesus? How have my experiences and prior training played into the opportunities in front of me to partner with Jesus?

Rather than building new programs (although that could be necessary after you assess needs), a better place to start is by asking diagnostic questions to help understand how God may want to grow the people you lead. For example, if a group of new believers have recently joined you and they don't know how to study their Bible, they may need a Bible study environment to supplement belonging. Those who have been a part of the church for twenty-five years and study their Bible consistently but struggle to have deeper relationships in the church should likely join a group centered on community or fellowship. When we assume everyone is at the same place spiritually and needs the same thing, we miss out on what is needed in the moment to create movement toward following Jesus.

No matter the environment, discipleship can only go so far as the relationship takes it, and belonging in those relationships is essential to formation. Todd Wilson writes, "For centuries, ordinary Christians have understood that profound personal and spiritual transformation happens not as much from know-ing as from being known. A new generation of neuroscientists are helping us to see this more clearly."[5] Wilson is referencing recent studies that show "our brains draw life from our strongest relational attachments to grow our character and deepen our identity. Who we love shapes who we are."[6] This increasing field of research shows that healthy relationships are key to lasting transformation. It is hard to overstate the importance of providing these types of environments in our church body. It is not enough just to provide these opportunities; we must also lead and challenge them to be intentionally pursuing relationships.

Discuss

1. Have you ever led a group (or talked with a group leader) where there was no clear purpose related to the overall goal of the church? Did that make leadership more difficult?

2. Have you ever noticed a new idea affecting someone to consider a truth of the gospel?

3. Do you agree that community is core to Christian discipleship? If yes, how have you experienced that in your life?

4. Do you spend more time in passive teaching environments or active ones? Why is that?

5. If you are a pastor or leader in the church, what kind of environments do you tend to create?

6. How do you find it difficult to trust others? How will you work to build trust among your group members?

7. How do you experience Jesus dynamically as you live?

8. Discipleship can only go so far as the relationship takes it. What are some practical implications of this?

CHAPTER 3

Groups as Deep Community

AS MY WIFE AND I (Justin) were preparing for marriage, we listened to a pastor talk about expectations and dreams in marriage. He said, "All the dreams and hopes you have for your life—where you're going to live, what kind of house you want, how many kids you want to have, and so forth—become expectations as soon as you walk back down the aisle after saying 'I do.'" Unspoken and mismanaged expectations in marriage lead to hurt and disappointment, and your group ministry is no different.

So, what can we promise in a group . . . really? Not much. In fact, we may fail you. We may hurt your feelings. Not by intention, of course, but because we live in a fallen world. We can't promise you will find all your best friends. But we can promise the opportunity for *the crowd* to shrink just a little. That's a start. But the possibilities are so much more than that.

When fifteen or so members of a group are present, there are fifteen different expectations for what the group will be, and often this includes a mixed bag filled with both good and difficult past experiences. These different expectations will all come to bear its weight on the group if unaddressed.

GROUPS AND EXPECTATIONS

Again, *groups are an art, not a science.* Your disappointment in community could actually be God's gift to you. Read that sentence again. Expectations, and missed expectations, are often gifts. Why? That disappointment points to something deeper. It reveals to you what may be under the surface driving your actions and reactions. These disappointments, if never addressed, will continue to haunt you, confuse you, and keep you from the community you so badly desire.

We are made by God to be in community, but if we aren't careful, "those who love [the] dream of a community more than the Christian community itself becomes the destroyer of the latter."[1] When our expectations get in the way of true biblical community, it's a gift to end up frustrated, because frustration often leads to change.

Leaders, as you lead your group, you have to realize on the front end that those *unspoken expectations (from both you and your group members) will keep your group from becoming the very thing it's intended to be.* No one wants to join a group they feel is a waste of their time. No one is looking to give up their Tuesday night with nothing in return. Both leaders and members are looking for something deep and transformational.

As a leader, you are creating an *opportunity* for biblical community, but you also are sure to run into the age-old ministry problem: you have more responsibility than you have authority. You can't make anyone change, and you can't be Jesus for them. Psalm 23 says, "The LORD is my shepherd; I shall not want." Jesus needs to be the Shepherd of the flock. He meets the needs and transforms His flock. We are just a small part of the process.

How do you love one another? First, by experiencing the Lord loving you. You can't give what you don't have. We don't love, encourage, or show mercy to one another naturally. The Lord has to be our Shepherd too. When you are following His lead, you are better prepared to minister to those in your group.

So, what can we truly promise to a group? Our friend Bill Willits shared with us the following considerations.[2]

- **Groups can be a path of connection for *most*.** Jesus often brought a crowd, but the crowd had little "skin in the game." They showed up and listened but didn't really participate or share. It is not unusual to have similar group members.

They likely are hit or miss when it comes to attendance, and even if they are in the room, they never seek to go deeper. Our opportunity, as leaders, is to rejoice in their first step to be a part of the group *and* to invite those on the edges into something deeper. In this we approach them like Jesus. "When he saw the crowds, he had compassion for them, because they were harassed and helpless, like sheep without a shepherd" (Matt. 9:36). Often sheep don't know they are being shepherded, and they certainly don't acknowledge that they need someone to do so. Those on the outside of your group may not know the opportunity in front of them to experience deep community, but you do. Labor to bring them fully into the fold.

- **Groups can be a path to growth in community for *many*.** Growth in biblical community is not reserved for the few. Many, and some would argue all, will grow in learning how to follow Jesus by being a part of a group. These group members are active participants, mirroring the deep community found among Jesus and His disciples. They had access to Jesus in ways and participated in ways the crowd did not and could not. These group members use their gifts for the building up of the body of Christ and grow and are shaped to look more like Christ, becoming more prepared for what the Lord has prepared in advance for them to do. Discovering, developing, and deploying spiritual gifts are key tasks for groups that lead to growth.

• **Groups can be a path to intimate community for *some*.** Most people join a group desiring intimate community, but fear, insecurity, schedules, or conflict may stand in the way. Leaders must do their best to remove any obstacles to intimacy but also find the few who can grow into a deep, gospel community. This is usually done within proximity and presence. *Proximity* is informal: we see one another around town, at the playgrounds, on a walk, or in the grocery store. *Presence* is more formal: we are intentional to see one another often and shape our lives around our community. While we can't develop this type of relationship with everyone, we've all found our people in larger crowds or groups at times, and it is a gift of God.

It's important for the leader to see the *group within the group*. If you don't, you will get frustrated and think you have failed, when in actuality you are doing exactly what Jesus did: involving the crowd, serving those who are engaged, and diving deeper with a smaller group. Everyone will not be like the three (Peter, James, and John). They experienced certain things together that the other twelve did not. And even within the three, Jesus had a special relationship with the one, John. The group within the group are those who are truly "in," not in a clique sense but in the sense of spiritual intimacy. This is a move from being "in a group" to doing life with one another. The group within the group becomes the invitation for those on the outside to experience something deeper.

- **Groups can be a fruitful experience for *anyone*.** In every group, conditions exist for a community of disciples to show others that the Father sent the Son to be the Savior of the world. God has a purpose for every group and for every person in a group, and the goal, no matter the depth of intimacy, is fruit. God is always working for the good of those in your group.

Now we know we have been trying to temper your expectations about what a group can promise, but we also want to encourage you in the opportunity of what a group can accomplish in your life and the lives of those in a group.

The people in your group are a partial inheritance from the Lord right now. Too often when we think about the inheritance we receive from the Lord, we think of it as some far-off future. That is good, right, and true, but God has also given you a portion of your salvation right now in the saints. He is so good to us!

The people in your group are a partial inheritance from the Lord right now.

Many in your group will never experience this portion because they don't know it exists or are unwilling to access that portion of their inheritance available now. What an amazing opportunity we have to help them open themselves to it. This is a sacred work.

So, what can we promise in a group . . . really? Jesus. His presence in other believers is something we can promise. What possibilities!

GROUPS AND VULNERABILITY

Community speaks to the deepest questions we have as humans. Who am I? Who is God? How do I relate to Him? Where is my place in this world?

As we said in the last chapter, over the last twenty years an increasing amount of research makes clear what we already knew: that we were made for connection. We were made for community, to be fully known and to be fully loved. Yet, for many of us, this has not been our *lived* experience. Past relational wounds or lived experiences make us withdraw from others.

The importance of community in the body of Christ helps us interpret our past experiences to find freedom, hope, and healing. We have been hurt in community (whether within our family of origin, due to past relational breakdowns, or other wounds inflicted by others), and we are healed in community.

The question is whether we will open ourselves up, knowing we could potentially be hurt again. Will we allow others to see us? Vulnerability is a step of faith. It's a step of courage.

But there is a difference between transparency and vulnerability. **Transparency** is showing the 95 percent, but vulnerability is showing 100 percent. Transparency is showing what I want to show you. But I'm not defenseless. **Vulnerability** is showing what I do not in my flesh want to share with you. Transparency is laying down some armor. Vulnerability is handing another the sword. Vulnerability necessitates courage because we invite the risk that we may be hurt by another. And yet, at the same time, it is the only pathway toward true belonging, deep connection, and the friendship we are made for.

There are two primary reasons we don't enter into deep community with vulnerability.

1. We don't think we need others.
2. We don't think we are good enough for others.

Vulnerability helps us walk over the threshold to face these two primal reasons that cause us to hesitate, laying it down so that we can be deeply known, sharpened toward looking more like Jesus.

We Don't Think We Need Others

The gospel says that community is a place to be needy and needed. Remember, *the less relational your church is, the less transformational your church will be.*

The gospel says that community is
a place to be needy and needed.

This is the first time in the history of humanity that you go to bed thinking mostly about you, yourself, and your problems. Throughout human history, people went to bed thinking about the problems of your village:

- Will we have enough food for the winter?
- Will we be protected from our enemy?

Your identity was shaped by the group identity of the village. Your neighbor's problems were your problems.

But not us, especially here in the West. Those in other cultures would see our focus on individualism as isolationism, but it's our chosen way of life. Calling it isolationism hurts more, doesn't it? We *know* being isolated is detrimental to our physical, emotional, and spiritual health. Everything around us tells us we are enough, we can make anything happen if we work hard enough, to follow our dreams. It's a crushing weight. You feel it. I feel it.

Not only does the gospel beg us to be needy and to be needed, but it also begs us to understand that we can't do it alone. We can't hold the weight of the world. We need Jesus, and we need someone outside of ourselves to remind us, day in and day out, that we need Jesus. This is what community does for us.

We Don't Think We Are Good Enough for Others

Sometimes we aren't able to engage in deep community because we don't think we are worth other people's love. We have thoughts like:

- If only they knew . . .
- If only I was a better Christian, I could . . .
- If only I didn't struggle with . . .

How would you finish those sentences? Do you worry about how those in your group would finish those sentences?

We all have narratives about ourselves running through our head. Some are true; others are not. When those stories condemn us, we often think people around us look at us with the same condemnation.

Your identity—who you believe you are—is shaped by your past experiences, memories, and wounds. Research shows us our brain processes our identity six times a second.[3] This is why false stories (lies) we tell ourselves are so important. If repetition is the mother of all learning, then the stories we tell ourselves, subconsciously rehearsed six times a second—roughly half a million times a day—are forming us. The question becomes: Do we have the right story? Do we have the right identity?

Of course, we are only able to scratch the surface in this chapter. This is a deep, lifelong journey we all have to decide to take. We are changed from "one degree of glory to another" (2 Cor. 3:18). It's almost always slower than we would like. Making space for you and others in your group to share deeply is a critical step in the process toward health in community.

Consider asking questions like:

- What is it like to be in community with me?
- When do you see me shut down?
- When do you see me get most excited?

These are the types of questions that can help bring about self-awareness. As one friend shared recently, "Self-awareness is a gift not everyone is given." That doesn't mean we can't grow into it. We have been hurt in community, and we are healed in community.

A quick word of caution is needed before we proceed: your story is your story, and their story is theirs. Some are not ready to share their deepest, darkest struggles with anyone, let alone a group. And honestly, it may not even be safe for them to do so. There are times when it's not a "lack of vulnerability." Sometimes, like in any sort of abuse past or present, it should be shared under the direction and supervision of a good counselor. The role of the group shifts to support and walk-forward care as needed.

How Does Vulnerability in Community Help Us Fight in Following Jesus?

Dietrich Bonhoeffer, in his seminal book *Life Together*, says this: "Sin demands to have a man by himself. It withdraws him from the community. The more isolated a person is, the more extractive will be the power of sin over him, and the more deeply he becomes involved in it, the more disastrous is his isolation."[4] Get that? Sin demands isolation.

In her book *The Gospel Comes with a House Key*, Rosaria Butterfield says, "It is an act of violence and cruelty to people in your church who routinely have no place to belong, no place to need and be needed, after worship. Worship leaves us full and raw, and we need one another."[5]

So, how do you expect her to finish her thought? Pray with them? Have intense Bible study together? Anything else? These are all good, but sometimes it's much simpler than that. She finishes her thought: "Know that someone is spared another spiral binge of pornography because he is instead playing Connect 4 with you or walking the dogs or jumping on the trampoline."[6]

We join in the spiritual fight together, pushing back darkness, when you do ordinary things with one another. Without vulnerability, sharing doubts, struggles, questions, testimonies, we won't even know when it's time to press in and when it's time to play Connect 4. This means we have to be courageous to share, but it also means we need to be a safe place to receive vulnerability from another.

Group leaders are crucial to creating a safe place for the healing to begin in a local church. *So goes groups, so goes the church. So goes the church, so goes groups.* A wise leader will remember the obstacles a member of a group has overcome to take the step of courage to be fully known.

The end of community and the fruit of vulnerability, as Jennie Allen would say, is to "find your people and, together, we build safe beautiful outposts that offer the love of God."[7] This is the holy work we do as groups of people meet together, surrendering their expectations and subjecting their vulnerabilities. Groups are ground zero for deep biblical community, and the call of God is to steward them well.

Discuss

1. What are some unrealistic expectations about groups that group members might have?

2. What are ways for the group to create clear expectations together?

3. In your experience, do people struggle to bridge the gap between transparency and vulnerability? How can you help them get there?

4. Have you found people in your group struggle with the ideas of being needy and needed?

5. How can you help your group members tell their own story while appreciating the differences in others' stories?

6. Does your church have a structure in place to help people who are working through past trauma? What if they were abused in church? What if it was your church? What steps should you take?

CHAPTER 4

Conflict and Confession

CONFLICT IS CRUCIAL, BUT few have experienced healthy conflict in their formative years. Putting together ten to twenty adults who never learned to resolve conflict in a healthy way has the potential to be explosive. Everyone has great intentions and gives the benefit of the doubt early in the life of a group. But then, after a little while, someone says something offensive, is noncommittal, or withholds himself or herself from the group, and conflict breaks out, hindering the spiritual growth the members need as well as the community they seek.

We all know conflict is part of life, but many of us are caught off guard when it springs up seemingly out of nowhere. In normal small groups, the question is not *if* the conflict comes but *when*, so we need to be prepared. When handled well, it may be the experience the Lord uses to increase intimacy and help the group grow into what He has planned for them. I don't know many people who love conflict management, but it is necessary for the growth of the leader and the members of the group to engage it when it arises.

"A CONFLICT IS A BLESSING IF . . ."

How would you finish that sentence? Maybe your first thought was, *if we don't destroy the relationship, or if we learn from this experience*, or maybe, *if we feel heard*. All of these are great answers. But remember, John 13:34–35 still bears its weight here. When Jesus tells us to "love one another," He is giving a command, which is an imperative in the Greek. As any parent will tell you, a command can be obeyed or disobeyed. This passage and many others must inform how we enter into conflict together.

We can't finish the statement above for you because every situation is dynamic, complex, and nuanced. But understanding that each of us has a family of origin that has shaped our experiences, temperament, and conflict style needs to be in the back of your mind as you help others enter conflict resolution. Conflict brings great opportunity for spiritual growth and relational intimacy. Most people lean out during these times of trouble and rob themselves and others of potential growth. Jesus says, "Love your enemies and pray for those who persecute you" (Matt. 5:44). Why? Because there is nothing distinctive about loving those who love you. That's normal, but the way of Jesus tells us to love those who are difficult to love because he has "[entrusted] to us the message of reconciliation" (2 Cor. 5:19).

Conflict is a result of the fall. It's "not as it should be." As followers of Jesus, we know that one day, one glorious future day, we will not have any relational conflict, tears, or suffering. Let's yearn for that day together and allow that eternal mindset to affect how we enter into conflict today.

Make a commitment in your heart, right now, before the conflict comes, that it will not undo the group. The Scriptures speak of a tethering of the people of God that roots us far beyond our human strength because the blood of Jesus and the power of the Holy Spirit draw us together. It should be nearly impossible to tear us apart. In a culture that says, "You do you," we can provide an alternative and be anti-culture by stepping into true forgiveness. When we forgive and are forgiven by others, we break the grip of the enemy and live in freedom.

How do we enter conflict well?

1. **Be a good listener first; then speak in love.** Ephesians 4:15 instructs us to speak the truth in love. To speak well, you also must listen well. Bad listeners, by definition, are selfish listeners, so strive to be humble. When you listen, you earn the right to be heard. Ask clarifying questions until you understand what's being said and can repeat it back accurately. Only when you hear clearly and understand can you expect others to hear what you have to say.

Below is a framework for questions we've found helpful as we walk ourselves and others through conflict. First, a few basics for mediating:

- Only one person may share at a time, and the person listening may only ask clarifying questions like, "This is what I hear you saying. . . . Is that right?" This is not a time to defend but to listen and understand.
- The questions below are progressive in nature, with each point building off the previous question. Walk through the process in order.
- The job of the mediator is to set up the time and enforce the rules.
- This is not recommended for a long-standing, ongoing, or complex situation where counseling sessions would be a better fit. This is better suited for on-the-ground, situational scenarios.

Hope

- What do you hope for this time? What do you hope for this relationship? I hope and look forward to . . .

Data

- What happened? Keep it to the facts.

Feeling

- How did it make you feel?

Judgment

- What judgments or conclusions have you made about the person or situation? What assumptions have you made that may or may not be true?

Lies

- What lies are you believing, or what sin have you committed? What do you need to own?
- It's possible to extend forgiveness before the other person opens their mouth.
- "My part in this is . . ."

Want

- What do you want?
- "The most important thing I want you to know is . . ."

Lastly

- "The story I'm telling myself is . . ."
- "Am I missing something, or have I gotten something wrong?"

Remember, this is just a process. This isn't a magic formula, and conflict will always be messy. Use discernment and a multitude of counselors to help you pursue health in any situation.

But know that your groups (and your church) will likely be better for it.

As you walk through these questions, remember that there's always a reason people respond the way they do. Every action has an equal and opposite reaction. Have you ever been in a conflict with someone and thought, *Goodness, this isn't THAT big of a deal. Why are they so upset?* For most people, the larger the reaction, the larger the reason behind that response. Being a good listener means asking, "Would you be willing to share more about how I offended you?" Paul Tripp is helpful here. He says, "Both truth and love matter. Whenever I am willing to speak hatefully to you, I step outside of God's way of communicating and destroy unity rather than build it. Whenever I am willing to compromise honesty, and I try to fool you into thinking we are unified, I create an illusion of unity that will soon blow up in our faces."[1]

Jesus is our peace, and He came both to build unity and to tear down walls. "For he himself is our peace, who has made the two groups one and has destroyed the barrier, the dividing wall of hostility" (Eph. 2:14 NIV). Don't rebuild a wall between you and another that Christ already destroyed.

2. **Desire to solve the problem rather than to win.** Emotionally and spiritually healthy people don't fight to *be* right. They fight for what *is* righteous. There is a world of difference between those two statements. So, are you the type of person who has to be right? If so, you will struggle to reconcile with others. The person you are in conflict with is not your enemy, so don't treat them as one. Desire to solve the problem rather than to win.

AS FAR AS IT DEPENDS ON YOU, LIVE AT PEACE

At times reconciliation and forgiveness mean different things to different people. You cannot force someone to reconcile, nor in certain instances is it safe to do so. Sometimes it is necessary for the safety of a person to completely break from a relationship and pursue forgiveness separately than return to a former situation. Escaping abusive or otherwise toxic relationships generally means involving others who have your best interest at heart, so lean in, include others, recommend counseling, or call authorities as it is warranted, and seek to show the love of Christ. In all situations, the call is to love one another.

One day we will all stand in front of the Lord and give an account for how we treated others with whom we experienced or mediated conflict. What did you do and what did you say? As we said earlier, this eternal perspective matters.

As leaders, there's nothing more important than this: it is *always* better to keep a short account than to allow bitterness and anger to fester between you and another saint.

GROUPS AND CONFESSION

The Christian life together isn't authentic unless it is marked by repentance together. While we've discussed the command to love one another extensively, this "one another" is also commanded: "Therefore, confess your sins to one another and pray for one another, so that you may be healed. The prayer of a righteous person is very powerful in its effect" (James 5:16 CSB). There is joy and freedom in confession and repentance when we do so with one another, but it is a concept riddled with real-world dynamics. Yet, with the varying dynamics, this one is unequivocally true: confession and repentance often cannot occur unless the group leaders lead out in it. As a leader goes first, whether in sharing his testimony or confessing his sin, he gives group members the gift of going second. A leader has the opportunity to model vulnerability, often bringing the group closer together and creating a space where confession and repentance are both understood and encouraged.

God uses confession and repentance to bring our sinful minds, hearts, and actions back to Himself every day. We continuously walk away from Him in our thoughtlessness and rebellion, yet God's gifts of confession and repentance allow us to move forward to follow Christ.

Before we discuss practical ways to lead your groups into meaningful confession and repentance, first we must define what confession and repentance are, as well as what they are not.

Confession is:

- Agreeing with God and admitting that we don't know best (Prov. 3:5–8).
- Beyond simply our actions and words to the heart (Rom. 10:10).
- About following Christ (2 Cor. 10:5).
- Healing (James 5:16).
- Involving your community (James 5:16).

Confession is not:

- Merely listing our sins before a pastor, a group leader, or a friend.
- Primarily about sin and our bad decisions.
- Admitting generally that we are sinful.

Repentance is:

- Rejecting sin and turning to God's transforming love (2 Cor. 7:9–10; Rev. 3:19).

- Turning away from sin and self to the gospel and God (Rom. 2:4).
- Turning from the commitment to sin to the commitment to God's kingdom (Matt. 4:17).
- Turning to God in a way that affects our lives deeply (Matt. 3:8).
- Pursuing godly sorrow rather than a worldly sorrow (2 Cor. 7:9–10).
- Running *to* God with our shame rather than running away (2 Pet. 3:9).

Repentance is not:

- Feeling bad about something because we think God is mad at us.
- Trying to dissect sin and understand it completely.
- Trying to stop a behavior without addressing the heart issue behind it.

How to encourage confession and repentance:

- Model it through your own vulnerability and admittance of your need for grace.
- Teach the basic truths of confession and repentance (as listed earlier).

- Pray for God to call the members of your group to confession and repentance.
- Make time and sacred space for confession, repentance, and prayer during group meetings. Gather women with women and men with men if that helps create a more conducive environment.
- Take care to guide people with the way they confess, keeping the focus on Jesus and not sin.
- Don't stop at confession. Lead confession to repentance and on to joy.

This last point is where 2 Corinthians 7:1–16 is an intensely practical passage for spiritual leaders. Paul is speaking to his spiritual children at Corinth, talking of past missionary endeavors, the reaction to his earlier strong letter, and how believers in Christ should conduct themselves. What Paul commands of the Corinthians, God still commands of those who follow Him.

We can pick up in the middle of his encouragement:

> I now rejoice, not that you were made sorrowful, but that you were made sorrowful to *the point of* repentance; for you were made sorrowful according to *the will of* God, so that you might not suffer loss in anything through

us. For the sorrow that is according to *the will of* God produces a repentance without regret, *leading* to salvation, but the sorrow of the world produces death. For behold what earnestness this very thing, this godly sorrow, has produced in you: what vindication of yourselves, what indignation, what fear, what longing, what zeal, what avenging of wrong! In everything you demonstrated yourselves to be innocent in the matter. So although I wrote to you, *it was* not for the sake of the offender nor for the sake of the one offended, but that your earnestness on our behalf might be made known to you in the sight of God. For this reason we have been comforted. (2 Cor. 7:9–13 NASB)

This passage is worthy of discussing early in the life of your group. In your initial time together, describe one of the goals of the group as an open place for confession, repentance, and the joy that comes with godly grief over sin. Lead your group in how to listen for worldly sorrow as well as godly grief that leads to repentance and restoration. That's a crucial distinction. Here are some pointers from Paul's teaching that cultivate discernment for our times of confession, repentance, and leading one another in them:

1. **Godly grief produces a repentance that leads to salvation without regret.** There can be pain and discomfort in bringing sin into the light, but it is clearly God's call for His community of believers. While we grieve our sin together, there's also earnestness for restoration and a renewed commitment to holiness. There is comfort in tour godly grief because we carry it and stake it rightly on the finished work of Christ together.

2. **Worldly grief produces death. Worldly grief results from sarcasm, passive aggressive (or just plain aggressive) words and behavior, or gossip arising from a wrong suffered.** We live in a fallen world where we both sin and are sinned against. Worldly grief is only concerned with finding fault or shame, but godly grief is seeking restoration. Sharing about a wrong should be done honestly, but we need one another to help us know when we have crossed the line into worldly grief in our descriptions.

This is definitely messy stuff. But isn't that why we signed on, group leaders? This is ultimately the *good* stuff. You cannot bypass the messiness of relationships. There is inherent risk involved in trusting and hoping with a group of people, but there is also growth in the tension and experience together. Enter into this good work and prepare your group to do the same.

Worldly grief is only concerned
with finding fault or shame.

Discuss

1. Have you ever been in a group where there was obvious conflict between group members? How did it affect the rest of the group?

2. Have you ever had to mediate conflict between group members? What are some specific things in this section that can help you?

3. How can you help foster an environment in which group members are willing to work through conflict productively?

4. How can you prepare the group for the messiness that accompanies confession of sin?

5. Have you been in a group where confession and repentance of both outward and hidden sin happened regularly? How have you sensed an authentic work of God in shared confession?

6. Is the above step-by-step guide enough to make you feel equipped to handle confession and repentance in the group? If not, schedule a meeting with a leader at your church to work through any gaps.

SECTION 3

The Group Life Cycle

CHAPTER 5

Groups Begin and End

A FEW YEARS AGO, we sat in a roomful of group leaders who had led what we assumed were incredibly healthy groups. One group in particular was known for loving one another deeply and serving those in their community, and it was clear the group had grown immensely through the years in their relationship with the Lord. The leaders of this group were beginning a new season of life with their kids and felt it was time to step away from leadership, so they asked their group hoping someone else would step into leadership.

Crickets.

While no one wanted the group to end and everyone saw it as a crucial part of their life, no one was willing to step up and lead for a season. As these leaders told their story, something dawned on us. We had failed these leaders. We had failed this group.

In our experience, the most spiritual growth occurs in the first eighteen months of a group, with diminishing returns after those eighteen months. This may be due to a number of factors. We tend to grow in our relationship with the Lord most when we take a step of faith and share vulnerable aspects of our story, confess present sins for the first time, and are forced out of our comfort zone. These are all part of the gift of a being in a group, but over time the stretching and sharpening that happens as groups share and grow, the feeling of intimacy can turn into complacency.

These groups become like a stagnant pool of water. There are bacteria plaguing the water because there's no fresh water flowing in or out, making it useless. It doesn't breed life; it breeds death. An indicator of stagnation in groups is a lack of change in a group in the last eighteen to thirty-six months. We want to breathe life into groups by presenting new opportunities for individuals to grow and change. It's a stirring up of the water in the pool—a check of the intake and exit so that the gospel might flow in, through, and out of groups. We do not want stagnation in our groups; we want the natural overflow of Christian discipleship: multiplication.

Healthy groups have a beginning and an end. But what happens in between? Will the group have a healthy progression or fizzle out along the way? What exactly is a healthy ending?

Groups are an art, not a science, and their development is far from linear. However, most groups experience stages along the way together. Naming those stages as you go can help map the journey toward growth and transformation. However, a map is only helpful if you know where you are *and* where you need to go.

Good leaders can read the map and recognize that their leadership has to change throughout the life cycle of their group. Every stage is different, requiring different skills, and some stages may feel more natural for you to lead than others. The recognition that you are leading in a space that doesn't come naturally may help you name the frustration you are feeling in the moment. Many leaders burn out because they are leading in a space where they are not gifted to lead. Again, that's okay; it won't last forever. You can ask for help from your church's leaders or delegate some responsibilities to those who are gifted in that space.

However, more than gifting or skills or leadership, "a leader's commitment to the group is one of the strongest predictors of a group's effectiveness and growth."[1] It's not all on you and your abilities. God does His best work with those who are willing to step in, listen to His prompting, and take steps of obedience to do His work.

In the following section, you'll find the fruit of working with other groups pastors to detail the life cycles of groups. Every stage will have a **name** and **statement** and will detail the **spiritual gifts that thrive** in the stage, as well as **how to transition out** of the current stage.

God does His best work with those who are
willing to step in, listen to His prompting,
and take steps of obedience to do His work.

STAGE 1: INCLUDE

Stage 1 is marked by inclusion. As a group initially comes together, the members are looking to the leader to identify what is acceptable behavior and what to expect. At this point members are *dependent on the leader.* Many times the leader makes the mistake of being too passive or too dominant. Leaders who are overly dominant run the risk of keeping members at arm's length, making it difficult for them to engage in the group or have a sense of ownership. However, if the leader is overly passive, the group tends to take on a life of its own, even spinning in confusion about why they exist. If everyone has their own idea of what the group is, it won't have the necessary cohesion needed to establish healthy rhythms.

Many are not ready to share their deepest darkest secrets the first night of a group, which is to be expected. It's the leader's job to provide a safe place for the journey of sharing to begin. We are setting the stage for trust to be built. Naturally, members of a group will test the waters with "small things" to see how they are handled before trusting the group with "big things," or, "according to Osterhaus, 'Trust is gained like a thermostat and lost like a light switch.' A leader builds trust slowly over time by constantly monitoring the conditions and actions that create the climate of trust in the room."[2]

Stage Statement: Consistency breeds trust.

We have often heard it said that trust is built when you are able to say about someone else, "You are who you say you are, and you'll do what you say you'll do." This is true in the confines of your group, too. What is the group going to be about? What is the rhythm going to be? What is the purpose of the group? The members of the group are dependent on the leader at this stage. This is where simple tasks done with excellence can go a long way to help the group move through Stage 1. If you say you're going to send a follow-up email to the group, send the email. If you say you are going to send out a calendar for the next six months, then do it. It's hard to overstate the importance of trust. Without it the journey will end before it begins.

With building trust comes a need to emphasize the significance of meeting together consistently. It often plays out like this: the group has been together for a few months. It starts out with a lot of energy and excitement. Things really seem to be coming together. Then 7:00 p.m. on meeting night rolls around, and the texts start coming through: "We can't make it tonight. One of the kids is sick." "I can't make it tonight because I'm out of town for work, and my husband won't make it either." And on and on it goes. Now many times these are legitimate reasons. The emphasis I want to put here is not on the reasons but our *response* as leaders.

The members of the group are looking to you to identify acceptable behavior and expectations. Your instinct may be to cancel your time together that week because "only a few people can make it." This is a HUGE mistake. The group will lose momentum because by canceling the group time you are inadvertently communicating to the group that it's not a big deal to miss. We can always cancel.

If you aren't willing to hold the line as the leader, the members won't hold it for you. If *consistency breeds trust*, then hold the line and be consistent, even if just two people show up. This is still the family of God coming together to share life, or as Jesus said, "For where two or three are gathered in my name, there am I among them" (Matt. 18:20). This smaller expression becomes an invitation to those who had to miss. Certainly there are weeks that need to be canceled for all sorts of reasons. Life happens. But by holding the line and doing everything you can to meet together consistently, you are communicating to the group that you can't have community without commitment.

If you aren't willing to hold the line as the leader, the members won't hold it for you.

Leaders are casting the vision for what their group is going to be about the second they receive their roster and start communicating the why, what, where, and so forth about the group. If you are a groups pastor, lean in to this moment and help leaders have clear on-ramps, communication, and a discipleship pathway. Seeing the on-ramp for group life through the lens of assimilation and formation provides the opportunity to set healthy expectations for everyone involved. In this stage it is important to make sure everyone understands why the group exists. Many naturally skip over the *why* and start with the *what*, but the why acts as the fuel for the engine to continue firing through the highs and lows of the coming months of group life.

Spiritual Gifts That Thrive in Stage 1: leadership, hospitality, administration, and other people-facing gifts

Transition to Stage 2 when members gain a sense of belonging and safety.

Most groups naturally transition to Stage 2 after a few months of sharing stories and creating predictability. Members have a better understanding of what this group will be about and how they can engage.

STAGE 2: EXPERIENCE

Stage 2 is marked by experience. The group begins to gel, and members are comfortable sharing ideas and opinions. Community buy-in and shared ownership are the keys for this stage. Members begin to share their life in a deeper, fuller way. They don't just share their thoughts; they also share their doubts and struggles. You know you are in Stage 2 when members know one another well enough to pray for one another meaningfully.

As a group grows through Stage 2, the leader should begin to invite others to lead, delegating while also overseeing their leadership. Letting others share the load will safeguard against leader burnout.

In Stage 1 we talked about the importance of leaders avoiding being overly dominant or passive. In Stage 2 you may reap what you have sown, as dominance will often create a facade that makes stepping into a leadership role too difficult for others. It's hard to overstate the destructive nature of what this does to the group, as it limits the opportunities for multiplication. That is a pool of water ripe for stagnation.

We've heard the hesitation in potential leaders often. "We can't be like Steve," a gifted elder in our church. The pressure they felt was leading exactly as Steve had led with his gifts and abilities, but we don't want an army of leaders who are exactly the same. I responded by saying, "That's great news! We don't want you to be Steve. We want you to be you to the glory of God." They heard us say they could use their gifts of hospitality and mercy to lead their group. Here's what's difficult. Steve never intended to create a facade. He is just a highly gifted man. Those who are highly gifted need to go above and beyond to break down the barrier of leadership for future leaders.

Groups can and should look different depending on who is in the group. A group filled with those who have the gift of evangelism will look different from those who have the gift of teaching (and every other mixture of spiritual gifts). Why? Because gifts are given "for building up the body of Christ" (Eph. 4:12), and in using the gifts given to each, others may see the body of Christ most clearly.

Most potential leaders feel they need to be something they're not: an imperfect form of the leader they most respect. An understanding that God has equipped and gifted them differently and called them to use their gifts for the building up of the body is incredibly freeing. Leaders who feel free to lead will do so with better insight, courage, and inspiration. Inspiration is what will get us through the hard times as leaders. Leading through the lens of the gospel and your gifts creates space for others to use their gifts to honor the Lord.

Stage Statement: This is *our* group (shared ownership).

Spiritual Gifts That Thrive in Stage 2: leadership, hospitality, mercy, discernment, helps, wisdom

Transition to Stage 3 when members feel a shared ownership of the group and when vulnerability is consistently experienced together.

Generally, in the early stages of a group, you hear statements like, "I'm in a group with them." But as groups move toward Stage 3, you may begin to hear statements like, "I am a part of their life" or "We are really close with them." Before moving to Stage 3, we need to consider that this is a natural place for groups to grow stagnant. Many don't know how to develop deep relationships, so they share some details of their life but don't actually engage in vulnerability. Conflict has the potential to divide the group if it is not avoided. But, as we see in Stage 3, it is the opportunity for deep community to manifest.

STAGE 3: INTEGRATE

Stage 3 is marked by closeness, often demonstrated in deeper connections and emotional safety. Often groups are launched into this stage in the aftermath of a conflict, crisis, or confession of sin. The group begins to engage in more mature and open dialogue about real-life issues with honesty and vulnerability. The group recognizes the unique experience they have had together, and if that experience was conflict, they may acknowledge it as a catalyst for growth while hoping never to go through the experience again.

As the group adapts to the new realities of what they have walked through together, it's normal to transition into less "formal" group times (study, etc.) because of the shared experience and common trust they now have with one another. Truly you find beauty from ashes.

It's only a matter of time before you enter Stage 3. No one is immune from the woes of the world and the possibility that our lives may completely change in an instant from a simple phone call. Suffering is unavoidable and expected in our Christian life. It's often incredibly lonely, but it doesn't have to be. This is one of the beautiful aspects of group life—to be able to "rejoice with those who rejoice; mourn with those who mourn" (Rom. 12:15 NIV).

After a season of normality and recovery, the group may be ready to transition into Stage 4.

Stage Statement: Press into the mess.

Spiritual Gifts That Thrive in Stage 3: leadership, teaching, discernment, wisdom, mercy

Transition to Stage 4 when it becomes apparent that the foxhole experience has forged deep trust within the group.

Just as in Stage 2, there is the potential to grow stagnant in Stage 3 because the group wasn't able to establish the necessary trust to make it through the fire together. Often this is when a group dissolves, but it also can be the catalyst for a core group to emerge that can take the group to a deeper level. Due to a deeply moving shared experience, groups can become more cliquish and resist bringing in new members, which would keep them from transitioning into Stage 4. In these groups, protecting what they currently have in the group is the priority. This tends to be the start of a long, slow, downward spiral toward the group's losing its effectiveness in helping the members grow in following Jesus.

Healthy groups, on the flip side, see the forged community as something powerful to invite others into. The group easily transitions into Stage 4 when they begin working together to serve and love their neighborhoods and cities in ways that advance the kingdom of God.

Stage 3 groups can take a cue from Japanese Kintsugi art; it takes something broken (a vase or a pot) and puts it back together with gold, silver, or platinum to bind it and make it even more valuable than before. This is what stage 3 achieves in the life cycle of a group. Truly, beauty from ashes and strength from trial.

STAGE 4: EXECUTE

Stage 4 is the natural overflow of the gospel together as laid out by Jesus in John 13:35: "By this all people will know that you are my disciples, if you have love for one another," but loving one another is not an end in and of itself. This is gospel in *and* gospel out. Everyone is using their spiritual gifts for the building up of the body. Everyone is jumping in and leading in some capacity.

At this stage, when visitors come to the group, they may not know who the "leader" is.

At this stage in the life cycle, the group becomes a space to invite those who don't follow Jesus into the gospel community that now exists. Missional communities use "third place" as a missional rhythm to have the group frequent in their neighborhood or an area like a coffee shop, playground, or restaurant. They take this gospel community into this space where people naturally congregate. The key is to be intentional in those spaces, exhibiting the beauty of a gospel community together so that others may know you are disciples by your love. Remember, the Scriptures don't know a people of God who focus only on community or mission. Both are keys to group life.

Stage Statement: The gospel, together.

Spiritual Gifts That Thrive in Stage 4: leadership, hospitality, administration, faith, generosity, healing, prophecy, serving, evangelism

Transition to Stage 5 as the gospel community grows and the opportunity for new groups emerges.

Many groups end their journey here. Over time that sweet gospel-in and gospel-out community becomes something that declines in the stacking of priorities. Similar to the story at the beginning of the chapter, there's likely not a desire for it to end, but there's also not another leader willing to continue it. Mission drift occurs, and the goal of making disciples gets pushed aside while the group just hangs out.

This doesn't always have to be the case. Of course, there are exceptions, but by and large this is the experience felt by most. When leaders intentionally lead toward Stage 5 from the beginning, the group transitions into purposeful multiplication and a legacy worth pursuing.

STAGE 5: END

As leaders, your goal from the beginning is not to be the same group for longer than eighteen to thirty-six months. As you lead, you prepare your group to multiply by stewarding them well from the first night. Express the goal of multiplication and keep it front and center. Multiplication is the picture of groups done well. Ask God to incorporate Acts 2:47 into the DNA of your group: "And the Lord added to their number day by day." The end isn't to be mourned; it's actually a picture of health. Sometimes groups become three groups (a biblical idea). As we've said, multiplication is the natural overflow of discipleship. If your group has never multiplied, then you may have stagnated in one of the previous stages without your realization.

Every group has a beginning and an end. We have an opportunity to normalize the experience of a group ending. Though it's a hard concept for leaders to understand, and most leaders will naturally blame themselves, it's often not anyone's fault when a group needs to end.

We aren't leading groups for the sake of leading groups, right? We lead groups because we believe God uses them to shape and mold us into Christlikeness. If a group stops being useful for that purpose, it should end. Jesus says that if salt loses its saltiness it's lost its usefulness. On the other hand, if a group is too large for the space they meet in or overwhelms the local coffee shop or park so that the others there see them as a nuisance instead of the aroma of Christ, it's likely time to end the group and launch a few in its place. Sometimes the living room space, or lack thereof, makes the argument for you. New group leaders will usually be trained, have people connect to their group, and then start in a living room. Two of our group leaders expressed this idea well recently. They told us, "We wanted to invite new people in, but we didn't want people to get too comfortable. We wanted a sense of being uncomfortable in community, even if that means space constraints in the first few weeks." A full house often makes the multiplication point.

To end a group is a serious decision and should never be made quickly or by the leader alone, but it absolutely can be the right decision. View it as an opportunity to launch new leaders into their gifting, as most groups have those who believe in Jesus, have the Holy Spirit living in them, and are capable of leading a group. They are likely already leading in some way, too, but don't yet have the title. Train these title-less leaders to take notice of the spiritual gifts in the group. This is most meaningful when we take enough interest in others, allowing us to be specific. Be observant of those in your believing community. Who is quick to volunteer and serve others? Who models self-control in their words and actions? Who exhibits patience with those who talk perhaps more than their fair share?

Based on what you observe, offer concrete examples of how you have seen this person live out their faith. It's deeply encouraging to hear, "I saw God's grace at work when you did this or said that." Specific examples bless the hearer and show that you have taken a genuine interest in them. Encourage them to serve and use their gifts to edify the church, rather in groups or in another ministry.

Stage Statement: The end depends on the beginning.

Spiritual Gifts That Thrive in Stage 5: apostolic, leadership, wisdom, discernment, serving, hospitality

What groups do you want to lead? A group that's stuck or one that's thriving? Our sincere hope throughout this section is that you have been able to recognize a few experiences you have had in the past and reinterpret those memories. Naming the experience can help tame the wounds we carry. So, what about you? Do your groups tend to stagnate in any particular stage? Why?

The end result of a group is either multiplication or being dissolved. Either way, God surely used the group in some capacity to help group members and leaders alike follow Him more closely. This is a beautiful thing.

The constant refrain is that relationships don't have to dissipate just because a new group starts out of an existing one. One of our group leaders said it best: "It isn't that we won't remain in relationship with one another; it's just that our friendships are going to evolve. That's the nature of what we do as leaders, as people."

And as Christians.

Discuss

1. Do any of these stages present a challenge for your leadership? Which one(s)?

2. Do you currently integrate spiritual gifts into the ongoing ministry of your group? (Do you involve members in a way that uses their gifts?)

3. What steps will you take to prevent stagnation in each stage?

4. If you've led a group before, what is the biggest challenge to starting a new group during that eighteen- to thirty-six-month window?

SECTION 4

A Handbook for Groups

CHAPTER 6

Groups Gathered

"We are a new group, and God has been forming sweet relationships. Everyone is hungry for connection, and they have been vulnerable and authentic with one another. We have seen the men get together for men's issues, friendships formed through game night gatherings, women getting together for lunch and walks in between regular meetings, and men helping one another with home repairs or car repairs. Basically forming attachments and relationships outside of the group. It sounds mundane to say it out loud, but this is our group, and these things have really helped us. Feels like we are ready to be there for one another. We know life won't always be so simple, but these beginning days for our group feel like they're forging trust for us to face trials together."
—Group Leader Testimony

IN THE FOLLOWING CHAPTERS you'll find collections of thoughts centered on groups as they gather, groups as they love one another well, and groups as they do outward-facing ministry. They will include questions at the end of each section rather than at the end of the chapter. We hope these final chapters will be a helpful resource you can keep on a nearby shelf and reference often as you launch new groups, train new leaders, and encourage groups to take a next step in obedience together.

In this chapter we'll circle back to the importance of the place a group gathers before moving on to moments that occur within the group: developing appropriate rhythms and guiding the group in prayer, Scripture, and response to what happens in the broader church family through the preaching of the Word.

GROUPS AND PLACE

Place matters. A person or a people's story is impossible to understand apart from their place of origin and where they have lived life. We are an embodied people, living in a particular place at a particular time. Jesus emphasizes the good of our embodiment in His incarnation. He Himself was like us in every respect (Heb. 2), even in His attachment to a place. Where did Jesus choose to spend His time? This has something to say about how we should structure the idea of place in our groups.

The Gospels record the ministry of Jesus occurring in three key locations: public spaces, the synagogue, and homes. Each has an obvious twenty-first-century counterpart. In Jesus's time, the home was considered the foundation on which the rest of society was built. As went the home so went the society. Considered rightly alongside Scripture's teaching on the importance of family and home, it should stand out to us that Jesus placed a special emphasis on homes as a place of intentional ministry. The four Gospels record more than fifty instances of this. Later in His ministry, Jesus began to move away from primary ministry in the synagogue and public spaces, moving more to homes.

Home Is Where the Group Is

We are not setting out to prove that the home is a primary place of ministry and evangelism. Jesus Himself already did. Jesus's practice of proximity in the most personal of places *matters* for how we design groups. Ministry is often best done in community that allows intimacy. Small groups are our effort to do the mission of God as much like Jesus did as we can, and one way we can do so is by hosting groups in homes.

Jesus used the home to build relationships and heal others, thus allowing Him to demonstrate the power and truth He came to teach. The ministry Jesus did in homes was His apologetic in many cases. He used the opportunities made available to Him through the relationships He fostered and the miracles He performed to teach on matters of faith, law, grace, and a range of other subjects. As it was in Jesus's day and as it has the potential to be today, the home is a place set apart to build relationships and provide a healing presence so that others may be open to the truth of the gospel. Jesus's ministry in homes was a ministry of love. Such love in the most private of places was the most potent apologetic to an unbelieving world. It still is. When life is lived in such close proximity, others have a reason to wonder why we believe what we believe as they see belief lived before their eyes, and for them this place of intimacy and safety becomes a place of revelation.

> The home is a place set apart to build relationships and provide a healing presence so that others may be open to the truth of the gospel.

In Jesus's day, homes were places of hospitality and intimacy where the host would open up their heart like they opened up the physical door of their home to others. They were places for knowing others and being known in the context of family and friendships. For Christians, homes were a context for bearing burdens and, in many cases, the primary context for ongoing participation in Christian living and witness to neighbors.

We both learned in our theological studies that first-century Jewish homes were a place of belonging and hospitality, not only for those they knew deeply and lived among but also for other peoples or nations (those who were not God's people). Welcoming strangers wasn't the normal practice of the day, but it was the key apologetic in ancient Jewish culture. It still could be. It should be. Jesus clearly took advantage of homes to instruct, develop relationships, and perform miracles such that everyone present in the home left saying, "We've never seen anything like this!" So too is the possibility when we see our homes as a genesis in ministering as Christ has to the believer, to the lost, and to spiritual skeptics. This is the possibility of a gospel-centered community that meets in a home. We won't innovate a faithful way around this, and we are fools to think we ever could surpass the Master's plan of evangelism and ministry.

Whether the home is or should be the primary and most effective place for ministry in these postmodern times may depend on context. Certain urban areas will have a difficult time with such home ministry because people may not want others in their space. There may be safety concerns, or a cultural memory of having someone in your home may not exist. In such contexts the church building can be a sanctuary.

It doesn't take a program. It doesn't take a budget meeting. It starts personally, and it starts in your homes. Begin by opening your home for a community to be affected by Jesus.

Community Is Costly

> *"A group member's adult son has decided to choose Christ over his same-sex partner. This came after months of his attending our group and saying it was a safe place. Many nights a few of us stayed after to pray with him and encourage him in Jesus. So grateful for our leaders who open their home so that people experience the love of Christ."*
> —Group Leader Testimony

My (Jared) wife and I have lost wedding gifts and family heirlooms because of groups in our homes. We've personally welcomed people—even pastors—who struggle with their faith in God, who struggle with unwanted sexual attraction, who struggle with their situation or injustices that they face, and who struggle with deep grief and health defects. We've lost sleep and time and money; we know members of our church who've lost so much more than that but gained a brother or sister in Christ because of it. It doesn't take a program to minister the gospel like Jesus did. All you have to do is open your home and heart that God gave to you.

Francis Schaeffer writes, "And there is no place in God's world where there are no people who will come and share a home as long as it is a real home."[1] A compassionate, open home is part of Christian responsibility, and each family should practice it up to the level of their capacity. Jesus made no distinction between home and foreign missions—it was all evangelism to Him. Small groups are our attempt to regularly emulate this practice as a people after Jesus.

Place matters. It mattered to Jesus, and it should matter to you. That the home is a primary place of ministry mattered to Him. That's why small groups matter to your church body. When evangelism and ministry happen in homes, it seems scripturally and experientially more effective than when meeting elsewhere. That's the plan. That's the place. That's the why, what, and wonder of small groups meeting in homes. Home is where the group is.

When evangelism and ministry happen
in homes, it seems scripturally and
experientially more effective than
when meeting elsewhere.

Discuss

1. What are some of the challenges of meeting in homes? What are the benefits?

2. Have you met with a group that rotated homes for their meetings? What were the advantages and disadvantages?

3. How does trying to build community in homes versus a room in your church's building or a third place differ?

GROUPS AND RHYTHMS

"I am constantly amazed and pleased with how our group cares for the different members. Over the past year we've had job losses, deaths in the family, serious illness, operations, and more, and in every case the group rallies around those that need comfort, prayer, and help, providing it en masse because we were meeting regularly. So many ministry opportunities. No matter the season, the group adapted to care well for one another."
—Group Member Testimony

One reason we love groups is because they are so adaptable. A group of young married couples without kids can and should look different from those who have fifteen children under seven years old. Every group should take into consideration the life stage of the group, the makeup of the group, the context of the group, and the needs of the group.

Below we have mapped out a few different options for the rhythm of a group. These are not exhaustive but are usually the most meaningful.

Rhythms are important for thriving in life and ministry. They help build consistency and trust in one another. Group members know what to expect and can build habits around the rhythm the group is already experiencing together.

The *rhythm* of the group is only there to support the *growth* of the group. We have a tendency to get locked into the structure and forget about the relationship. If the structure isn't working, change it. When you pick your model (rhythm), you pick your problems and your opportunities. No model is perfect.

The *rhythm* of the group is only there
to support the *growth* of the group.

Family Discipleship Rhythm

Have you ever tried to lead a small group with twenty-plus kids? It can be a challenge, to say the least. Most group leaders and members try to do too much when they are in the season of life that involves sippy cups and sight words. They can easily burn out or find it difficult to establish a healthy rhythm as kids get sick or other needs have to take precedence. In our experience, creating a family discipleship rhythm helps alleviate the pressure of doing everything while giving direction for the community to bring kids into the group. Because, well, kids *are* a part of the group. In fact, if we are a part of a group together and you don't know my kids or how I respond to them (positively and negatively), there is an aspect of me you don't know. This is an aspect of vulnerability.

Here's a rhythm we've seen work:

Week 1: Women meet—men watch the kids

Week 2: Men meet—women watch the kids

Week 3: Family discipleship night with kids (might include family worship, craft, teaching, and so forth)

Week 4: Adults only (babysitter)

This rhythm, or one similar to it, creates opportunities for learning, serving, accountability, and transparency within families without breaking the bank or putting too much responsibility on a single leader.

Missional Community Rhythm

In this model the focus becomes missional in nature. The concept of a "third place" as discussed earlier creates rhythms around natural gathering spaces in the community. Examples include a coffee shop, playground, restaurant, or any other environment where people gather. The beautiful part is that the group doesn't have to change anything. They still do whatever they were going to do in their host home. The point of gathering is to build relationships with others who don't know Jesus. As we've heard it said, "People can *belong* before they *believe* in Jesus."

Historic Church Calendar Rhythm

Following the church calendar for a season can be a beautiful way of being formed together as a group. The historic church calendar has six distinct seasons:

Advent: the birth of Christ

Epiphany: the manifestation of Christ

Lent: the temptation and death of Christ

Easter: the resurrection of Christ

Pentecost: the Spirit and mission of Christ

Ordinary Time

Each of these seasons has different liturgy, practices, and traditions to help us refocus our lives around what Jesus is doing in the world.

Summer, December

Your group is your spiritual family, the people you do life with at a deep level. Share convictions and confession of sin. Mourn and rejoice together. But do take a "break" for the summer.

Wait, what?

It can be confusing to share life with a group of people and then not see them between June and August. Unfortunately, this is a mistake we see many make in groups ministry.

Naturally, groups tend to drop off during December and in the summer. It's hard to have any sort of consistency because of family trips, summer camps, and so forth. On the flip side, many leaders don't feel like they can or should take a break. They feel like they are abdicating responsibility for leading. We feel the same, but that doesn't mean the group can't change the rhythm they have during the summer and Christmas season. This is a perfect opportunity to delegate to others in the group and rely on front-yard barbecues and service opportunities to provide consistency of relationships without too much commitment. This also gives group leaders a little breather so they do not burn out over the long haul.

Sabbath

A word on Sabbath: many of us don't Sabbath well. We run and run and run until we redline or break down completely. Yet, Sabbath is given as a gift from God to help us embrace our limitations. Through Sabbath. We understand we are ultimately not in control and must actively trust God to do that which is beyond us. Think about this. Throughout the Old Testament God orders His people to party. He tells us to rest, to feast, to party! How great is that? He doesn't say, "You better produce something so you are worth something." He says to rest. There is a season to work and a season to rest. A season to rejoice and a season to mourn.

Sabbath becomes easier when we have accountability and take a weekly Sabbath together. Simply taking a night/day off (5:00 p.m.–5:00 p.m.) and beginning or ending Sabbath with a meal around the table with friends helps remind us of what is truly important in life.

Discuss

1. Which of the rhythms listed above is most appealing to you?

2. If you have led groups in the past, was it challenging to get everyone back together after extended breaks?

3. How do you personally observe Sabbath rest?

4. How will you lead the group to integrate Sabbath into your meeting rhythm?

GROUPS AND PRACTICAL PRAYERS

"Our group truly wants to follow the Lord with their whole lives! We have participated in fasting together and praying together. We also share very openly and honestly and have been able to go deep into one anothers' lives because we are praying more together."

"Our group has just been experiencing a heavy season—a lot of life and health issues. And because we're a mostly single

*women's group, we've walked through some sadness and
hardship around being in that season still. But we did just
experience a miraculous healing of the unborn child of one
of our couples! She was told that their baby would be born
with a disability, and so we had been praying and dedicated
a night to go pray over them and the baby. The next week she
had a scan, and the baby was totally healed. Such a joy! We
also have been experiencing more vulnerability in the group
because of prayer, and that has been sweet to see."*
—Group Leader Testimonies

Praying together in small groups involves listening to God
and one another. Often when group leaders ask about prayer
time, we want to encourage them to focus on small groups being
the primary place for such intercessory ministry to one another.
It is difficult in the larger Sunday morning gathering to connect,
share, listen, and pray together.

It's vital to remember the first-century context in which Paul
wrote his letters to the church. A plurality of house churches
existed at this time; usually growing to as large as any one house
could hold, probably maxing out at around 25 people.[2] Most
would have been far fewer and likely looked a lot like your
current small group size. Paul didn't write to large crowds but,
rather, sought to instruct smaller gatherings.

And these commands of God given to us through many of Paul's letters—particularly around prayer, intercession, and practice of spiritual gifts—are much easier to understand and implement in a small group where virtually everyone knows everyone else. Thus, personal situations, gifts, and prayer needs would be more intimately known as well. This gives us a greater chance of making our groups a consecrated place of personal ministry in prayer. All it takes is creating space.

God's Holy Spirit is the true leader of every group. The group leaders are men and women who listen to Him and provide shepherding, but He is the ultimate Shepherd. As the group seeks to follow the Spirit's leading, leaders will need to create a safe environment for people to pray—out loud and over one another, asking for words of insight or encouragement to share. Our obedience is to make ourselves available and to ask in faith. See what the Lord will do.

Creating space for a consistent ministry of listening and praying in your group helps people know they are loved, valued, and invited to get into what God is doing in the lives of those in the group. When we pray for one another, we contribute. We step out in obedience and gain courage together, and our faith is increased as we honor one another in doing so. And often we see prayers answered!

But if we do not create such space for intentional prayer over one another in small groups, we can't expect it to happen. Time for prayer must be built into the structure of your meeting time and shouldn't just be the transition from fellowship to study or the way to signal the end of the group time.

Are you open to creating space in your weekly group meeting that makes prayer the central aspect of community with God and one another?

Could it be risky? Yes. It might be silent for a while; maybe it needs to be. How often do we really pause in quiet for two minutes or five minutes? What would it look like to create this oasis of silence and stillness, asking the Spirit to reveal, heal, and move in our group time every time we meet? The Spirit's interruptions are the ones we want!

Creating the space for prayer not only helps with groups being orderly but also makes a regular opening for personal ministry to one another. Maybe this time practically starts with repeating James's invitation to your group each week: "Is anyone among you suffering? Let him pray. Is anyone cheerful? Let him sing praise. Is anyone among you sick? Let him call for the elders of the church, and let them pray over him, anointing him with oil in the name of the Lord. And the prayer of faith will save the one who is sick, and the Lord will raise him up. And if he has committed sins, he will be forgiven" (James 5:13–15).

Then pray for one another as the Spirit prompts, prods, and behooves us. Invite your church's elders into small groups for such ministry. Let everyone get in on what God is doing in your midst. Every group time produces a fresh opportunity for ministry. God wants to do work in your group. All it takes is to create the space and ask. His Spirit will do the rest. That's about as practical as it gets.

Discuss

1. Have you considered discipleship in prayer part of a regular group function?

2. How frequently will you incorporate long seasons of group prayer (as opposed to only opening and closing with prayer)?

3. Does your church have specific practices for things like anointing with oil that might require pastoral involvement?

4. What are other ways (books, journaling, prayer partners) you can encourage prayer in the group?

GROUPS AND READING SCRIPTURE

There was a group in our church who made the book of Deuteronomy their group's reading one year. While not every small group leader's first choice, these leaders felt impressed by God to dive into this Old Testament law story and to make sure portions of it were read out loud by group members each week. They arrived about halfway through the book, and the group was reading out loud passages warning against bringing sin into the midst of believers and a command to purge such evil from the community. The Word of God read aloud resonated in the hearts of the group members that night. Under conviction of the Holy Spirit and these words simply being read out loud, three couples confessed to ongoing extra-marital affairs. The group moved in to care and began a road of reconciliation. The lives of these three couples were changed forever. Sin was confessed, repentance made, and healing could begin. All because the Word was trusted, read aloud, and the Spirit moved.

Personal Bible reading, meditation, journaling, meaty theology books—we like them. Sometimes they're just hard to translate into a community of varying interests, desires, life stages, and education. There is a place for your personal, passionate pursuit of God in reading, but the Bible is ultimately a community treasure. It was never meant to remain a solely singular endeavor.

Before it was inscribed on vellum and papyrus or downloaded straight to your smartphone, the stories, proverbs, and poetry of the Bible circulated orally, and even after the oral literature was written down, it continued to be transmitted orally. We both learned in our early Old Testament classes that literature in the ancient world was often read out loud.[3] This is still the case today in much of the worldwide church, and that is appropriate because the Bible was meant to be received aurally. That's historic and the most human way. The reading of the Word of God has always been a communal experience. Let your small group step into that ancient flow.

Scripture commands us to read the Bible out loud: "Devote yourself to the public reading of Scripture" (1 Tim. 4:13), and while this is central in a worship service, it can be central to your small group meeting, too. Reading aloud is intensely practical. We are forgetful people and all too often foggy in our thinking and heart's desires. The public reading of Scripture out loud clears the fog and reminds us of who we are, both individually and together.

We aren't just talking about Sunday morning liturgies. This includes Tuesday evening. Friday evening. Whenever the group is together, we start and base what we do in the sharing and hearing of God's own words. Read the week's preached Scripture passage or follow a reading plan or read entire books of the Bible together aloud. The Scriptures are still living and active, piercing and dividing us from our hidden sins in community.

Reading long passages together is right in line with church history. In the early church most New Testament books were read in one sitting together in community. Certain patterns and themes are revealed when a book is read outside of personal "fast reading." (Let's all be honest, we are increasingly scrolling readers. Don't treat Scripture like your social media feed or a blog post.) Don't miss what God has for you together. Slow down and listen to one another read.

You can split up passages by paragraphs, chapters, or dialogue. Listen to the voices God has put in your group as they take on God's voice through the reading of psalms, hymns, spiritual songs, and stories. This is a worship strategy for your small group. If you don't have a guitar player or a choir's collection of singers, let the voices you have all participate in the reading. We think you'll be moved by the chorus.

Hearing and seeing a reader embody the text is a different experience than silently pondering a Scripture in private study. Have you heard the Word read well? Vistas of new understanding and worship open as the people of God receive His words together. Reading the Word out loud in community need not be long faced and doleful. It can come alive with the voices of dear friends.

Discuss

1. How might you integrate Scripture reading more deeply into your group time?

2. List some ways to encourage your group members to read Scripture when you are apart.

GROUPS AND SERMONS

If preaching matters so much, what are we to do with the sermon in our small groups? For far too long we've placed preaching and community in separate silos. But clear, biblical proclamation must always be connected to community.

The first heart the preached Word must affect in your small group is *yours*. It *could* look this way: focus your Monday morning devotion on reviewing and rehearsing the preached Word you heard over the weekend. Take notes during the sermon and devote Monday's waking hours to living out the message God gave through His preacher. What was the Holy Spirit directing you to do out of the text? What spurred you on in holiness? What convicted you? What direction or conviction was given for you to encourage, confess, repent, reconcile, or reach out? Be faithful to follow up on these God-given directions; then share them with your community.

The outgrowth of your obedience to God's Word spreads directly into your gospel-centered community. Those with whom you walk are always affected by your decision to engage with and obey (or not) the message. John Wesley recognized that the need for church members to share their lives and convictions were not met in the large weekend service, so he purposed "band meetings," smaller groups of believers from within the church to encourage one another for holy living.[4] He saw these groups as

an outgrowth of Sunday's sermon, building into them an emphasis on application of the preached Word as members regularly
shared their spiritual condition, confessed sin and hardship, and
prayed together.

As churches preach through the books of the Bible, there is
a wonderful opportunity for us to be confronted with the same
Word of God, both as individuals and as a community. We can
create a culture of unity and authenticity as we lead our groups
to devote their shared study time to the books and passages
preached on the weekends. None of us are interested in developing connoisseurs of sermons but in making disciples passionate
about acting on God's call upon us.

Groups have the opportunity to increase not only gospel-
centered community but also gospel-centered multiplication
as they rally around the proclaimed message. Preaching and
community are not the end goals; making disciples is. Even as
preaching is to drive and direct small groups, the message doesn't
stop with the group. Together we constantly consider ways the
Word of God may multiply out into the souls with whom we
share a wider sphere.

As you meet, consider asking these questions to get group
members talking about the sermon and the ways they are seeking to live it out: What is God telling you to do? How can we be
part of giving you courage to obey? How can we pray for you?
For your neighbors?

Discuss

1. How does the message preached on Sunday affect your group?

2. Ask your group members how frequently they think about or refer to the Sunday sermon during each week.

3. What are some of the benefits of going over the sermon and its Bible text as a group?

CHAPTER 7

Groups and Loving One Another Well

"After ten years of history and suffering, a member
of our group has been declared cancer free. He was diag-
nosed and given three years to live. His wife left him for
another man. He's struggled and persevered. He said this
morning that his group has been instrumental to his hope
and endurance. 'Wouldn't have made it without them.
They made the true difference.' Perhaps his is a story you
can capture and share. It is just one of many."
—Group Leader Testimony

IN THIS CHAPTER, WE'LL cover the many aspects of the visual
outworking of the spiritual work God does through groups. It is
a gift to see members encourage one another, serve using their
gifts to a new degree, or fight off spiritual warfare with a new
fervor alongside one another.

GROUP CHALLENGES

Caring for one another isn't easy. The self-care craze comes at us pretty hard. Jeffrey Hall writes that these self-care regimes focus on "cultivation of a mindful, inwardly focused life. There are increasing efforts to cut out other people in the name of removing toxicity, and all these tendencies are pushed forward by frictionless technologies that remove social obligations to leave home, talk to others and engage in our community."[1] *There is no lasting transformation in a person without another person.* The danger is that the default is now "self-care" when souls need *"community care."* This can be how we currently fail the people God has entrusted to us.

Church hurt also makes us recoil from community. There is no hurt like it, and it can stop us in our tracks for a long time and make us withdraw. This may never be more true than in relationships of trust. We often expect human nature to be different among the people of God, but sometimes the group experience just isn't what we expected. A leader may face personal issues or an increasingly pressed or crushed capacity. Sometimes relationships of trust are outright betrayed or broken by besetting sin in one or both people's lives.

There's also the fear of intimacy. We are often more comfortable being side by side rather than face-to-face in friendships. Relationships of trust require vulnerability, but we have to dig deep at the shame of not always being in emotional control before we can cultivate. We live in a culture of competition; we are told to be strong and successful and run past anyone who gets in the way. There's a growing trend of defensive detachment. All of this must be faced if we are to play our part of the transformation God has for one another. *The less relational your church is, the less transformational your church will be.*

And we admit here that group can be exhausting. Regardless of your personality, interacting with other humans can be hard work. After decades of church membership and a combined forty years of leading groups, we've learned that church can be one of the toughest places to cultivate and retain relationships of trust. It can be overwhelming to try this over and over again.

Meeting the Challenge Moment by Moment

You may know the feeling; every group leader or group member does. It's Tuesday afternoon, just after 5:00 p.m., and you're headed home, poured out and ready to drop from the day. As you dream about how you will relax and introvert into the evening (even if you're extroverted, you're *that* tired), it hits you, and your stomach sinks.

"Oh, man. We have group tonight."

It happens to even the most devoted of us. It's normal from time to time to dread group meeting for various reasons, but we've learned to get concerned when that feeling becomes nor-mative in us.

So, how do you fight off what any seasoned group leader or member will tell you is bound to happen? You have to meet that feeling right at the moment it hits you at 5:00 p.m. or in the middle of group when you're wondering where the conversation is going. Meet that feeling of unfaith in your soul. Anticipate it and counter it with something it never expects, something deep and simple: a moment-by-moment faith.

Francis Schaeffer's *True Spirituality* paints the picture of the fight of the group leader and member:

> The Christian life is moment by moment. . . .
> As we believe God for this moment, the Holy
> Spirit is not quenched. And through His agency,
> the risen and glorified Christ, as the Bridegroom
> of the bride, the vine, brings forth His fruit
> through us, at this moment. This is the practice
> of active passivity. And it is the only way any-body can live; there is no other way to live but
> moment by moment. . . . And so it must be for
> us. We accept Christ as Savior at one moment,
> and our guilt is gone on the basis of the value of
> the finished work of Jesus Christ. But after we
> become Christians, the moments proceed, the

clock continues to tick; and in every moment of time, our calling is to believe God, raise the empty hands of faith, and let fruit flow out through us.[2]

The greatest thing you have to offer your group members and participants is your own personal relationship to and reliance on God. We should lead ourselves and one another in constant reminders to (1) believe God, (2) raise empty hands of faith, and (3) let fruit flow out through us and into our group participants. Sometimes this looks like praying for this faith on Tuesday at 5:00 p.m. Other times it means mentally reminding yourself (and then audibly reminding your group) that we are meeting because God exists, He has sent His Son to be the Savior of the world, and He wants to do work in and through us.

The win for your group isn't dependent on your ability. Your group depends on your dependency, your moment-by-moment faith. In the end, that will be your greatest investment in one another.

Groups and Encouragement

Therefore encourage one another and build one another up, just as you are doing. (1 Thess. 5:11)

Christian encouragement—or depositing godly courage into one another through our words and actions—is a command. Yet we find it counterintuitive in a world obsessed with petty cynicism. It may also seem awkward, or maybe we are just moving too fast to employ it in our daily life. It doesn't have to be uncomfortable, though. Like any other skill, we get better at encouragement with practice. A healthy group consistently dedicates time to "encourage one another and build one another up." With that in mind, here are five suggestions to help you grow in your ability to encourage others.

Turn to the Word. Not everyone is naturally comfortable crafting the perfect words for a given situation. In practicing encouragement, I have found that the fewer words I use of my own, the better. This realization has relieved me to encourage all the more and with greater truthfulness because I don't need my words to encourage—I need God's Word.

Let the Scriptures be your starting point for encouraging others. Share with fellow believers where you see the Spirit working in and through them. Point out the fruit of the Spirit you see growing in them (Gal. 5:22–23), and affirm them in their spiritual gifting and faithful use of those gifts (1 Cor. 12; Rom. 12). Celebrating someone's spiritual fruit and gifting is a good start toward true Christian encouragement.

Be Specific. Our encouragement is most meaningful when we take interest in others and are specific with our encouragement. Be observant of those in your believing community. Who is quick to volunteer to serve others? Who models self-control in their words and actions? Who exhibits patience with those who talk perhaps more than they should?

Based on what you observe, offer concrete examples of how you have seen this person live out their faith. It's deeply encouraging to hear, "I saw God's grace at work when you did this or said that." Specific examples bless the hearer and show that you have taken a genuine interest in them.

Be Intentional. Give thought to who could use encouragement. Our ministry teams set aside time during some of our team meetings to encourage one another. We choose an individual in advance of the meeting and spend time intentionally telling them how we see them being used by God specifically. It deepens us as individuals and as a community.

Whether we work for a church or not, we are all doing the work of ministry, and because it is difficult work, we all need encouragement. The best way to be intentional is to think ahead and praise someone based on where you see faithfulness and fruit of the Spirit in them. This intentionality goes deeper than a simple compliment. The goal is to call out where you see God's image in them.

Be Selfless. Have you ever held back from encouraging someone because you were afraid you might feed their pride? Have you ever withheld encouragement because you viewed someone as a rival in your work environment or your circle of friends? Maybe we all have, but Christian encouragement and flattery are not the same. In fact, they sit at opposite ends of the spectrum.

Don't let fear of being seen as a flatterer cause you to curtail your genuine words of encouragement. Don't let your own insecurities inhibit your praise of others. The one who encourages practices selflessness, taking the words of Proverbs 12:18 to heart: "There is one whose rash words are like sword thrusts, but the tongue of the wise brings healing." You can encourage someone for their benefit without flattering them for your own.

We have a choice to be selfish or selfless in our encouragement. We can either harm by the selfishness of our silence or diminished praise, or we can heal by the selflessness of our fruitful words driven by the Scriptures.

Be Courageous. Don't just encourage godly things already done, but encourage the pursuit of godly things not yet being done, as well. We often need godly courage to pass along godly courage.

If a friend is looking at pornography, find words to encourage them toward desiring Christlikeness instead of illicit images. If a friend is engaging in gossip, find words to encourage them toward Christ-honoring speech. Be gracious rather than legalistic, and seek to identify with your friend's battle, no matter the battle. Make sure your encouragement is loving. Use Christian courage to confront sin with kindness and gentleness.

We believe encouragement should take its place alongside any list of spiritual disciplines. We've found few exercises to be more challenging and yet so affirming to our walks with Christ and the ability to benefit our brothers and sisters than the ministry of encouragement.

When we encourage someone, we have the opportunity to speak healing truth into their life. We do this by grace through a heart changed by Christ and words drawn from Scripture. In this way, may we strive to excel in building up the church (1 Cor. 14:12).

Discuss

1. What is the most difficult thing about encouragement?

2. How can you personally encourage each member? How can you lead each member of the group to encourage the other members?

GROUPS AND GIFTS

"One woman has been freed of a lifelong addiction, another woman experienced a significant physical healing, several are sharing Jesus with coworkers and neighbors actively, and we have seen several professions of faith. One young man is pro-actively trying to disciple and shepherd all the younger guys in our group. God has been building a sweet community as many bring their giftings to bear in this group."

"I am just constantly amazed and pleased with how our group cares for the different members. Over the past year we've had job losses, deaths in the family, serious illness, operations, and more; and in every case the group rallies around those that need comfort, prayer, and help. It is such an amazing gathering of giftings in our group!"
—Group Leader Testimonies

It *is* amazing. Every group is full of gifted people. We believe that a small group environment is the best place to discover, develop, and even deploy those gifts in the local church. In fact, the group and the church of which it is a part cannot function without the direct empowering of the Holy Spirit for us to minister the gospel in community with God, one another, and to our neighbors.

What do all Christians have in common so far as belief and practice of spiritual gifts? We've seen across the spectrum and noted that nearly all affirm that the Holy Spirit does empower and endow believers with gifts to serve and build the church. Regardless of where a church or individual falls on the spectrum of continuationism (all the gifts mentioned in Scripture are still in operation) or cessationism (some of the gifts mentioned in Scripture have ceased), there are general truths about spiritual gifts all Christians can agree on. Sam Storms offers a definition we've found helpful: "Spiritual gifts are capacities or abilities imparted to Christians by the Holy Spirit to enable them to exceed the limitations of their finite humanity in order to serve other believers to the glory of God."[3]

Spiritual gifts imparted by the Spirit, natural gifts that overflow from God's kindness to all people, and acquired gifts that have been learned over time benefit groups greatly, and groups can help members discover their gifts together.

Illumination

A great exercise to do with your group is to read the primary chapters of Scripture that talk about spiritual gifts and pray for the Lord to reveal how He is using each of you. These key passages are Romans 12; 1 Corinthians 12; and Ephesians 4. The Spirit gives His gifts in order to meet needs in His church, so think about that as you read the following together out loud. Also consider:

- Romans 12 speaks largely of *motivation gifts*. These serve the church in substantial and supernatural ways that impact the everyday functions and ministry.
- First Corinthians 12 speaks largely of *manifestation gifts*. These are the gifts that often have great mystery and disagreement among believers. Acknowledge the mystery of it all and help group members see that these gifts are used most to testify God's power to both believers and unbelievers for the sake of building the church.
- Ephesians 4 speaks largely of *ministry leadership gifts*. These appear right in the middle of a chapter about oneness, and that's what these gifts are all about: unifying and building the kingdom of God. This purpose sets them apart from other kinds of gifts and talents.

Empowered

Each member of the group is born with natural gifts (or call them *talents* if you like). You're a good athlete. You take easily to complex math. You nurture others. Such natural gifts are indeed gifts of God because He gave them to you. They are to be stewarded and can even help direct us in our vocation. Recognizing them takes being honest about how you are wired and talented and listening to what others believe is true about you. Community is a great place to explore these gifts.

Each member of the group has acquired gifts they've picked up along the way. These can be from family experiences, education, access to information, or a job. These tools are also given by God and should be stewarded as such.

Both natural and acquired gifts can be used for the general good of people, but some bury them deep or don't use theirs because they don't realize their value. Groups can spur one another on to good works by calling out these gifts in one another, possibly gifts members didn't even realize they have or that they've worried it would be prideful to acknowledge. While these gifts are all given by God, people might use them to edify the church, or they may be used apart from God's kingdom.

Not so with spiritual gifts. Each member of the group who is a believer in Jesus Christ is given gifts directly from His Holy Spirit to further the kingdom of God. The major difference between spiritual gifts and the other two categories is that spiritual gifts, when truly employed, produce long-term spiritual joy in the person giving and the one receiving. They are only given to the church. Spiritual gifts exclusively and always further the kingdom. They can only be used for this purpose. You aren't born with them, though you are reborn with them. You can't acquire them. They aren't earned. They are truly gifts.

Spiritual gifts, when truly employed, produce long-term spiritual joy in the person giving and the one receiving.

All gifts—natural, acquired, and spiritual—should be used for God. But He is present *every time* a spiritual gift is used.

Every group is filled with gifted people. Consider your own group members in light of such gifts. If *groups exist for community with God and one another,* then they are also the best place to explore, practice, and serve with our gifts.

Integrate the Fruit of the Spirit

The point of gifts is Christlikeness and displaying the fruit of the Spirit as shown in Galatians 5. The point is not the gifts. They are a means to build up the believers and invite in yet more to believe and follow Jesus. The beginning and end of any gift's lasting impact is Jesus.

Compare any use of gifts—natural, acquired, or spiritual—with the fruit of the Spirit. Does the employment of the gift increase faith, hope, and love? Is there growth in long-suffering? Is there a measure of peace? Properly used *gifts* of the Spirit will produce more *fruit* of the Spirit.

Discuss

1. What are your natural gifts? Acquired gifts? Spiritual gifts? How are you using them currently?

2. Does your church use any tool to assist people in discovering their spiritual gifts? If not, how will you help group members discover theirs?

3. How can you lead members to serve in areas where their gifts are best used?

GROUPS ARE SPIRITUAL WARFARE

*"Spiritual warfare has increased ever since
we decided to step into leading a group."*
—Group Leader Testimony

We hear this fairly regularly from newly launched group leaders and also experienced it in groups we led. Don't be surprised by it.

As group leaders we are often at the front line of ministry in the local church. Of course, the enemy of God targets those leading His children into a space for community with Him and one another. There's nothing the enemy hates more than Christians joining together in unity. If he sees you getting along, developing deep relationships of trust, experiencing healing, using your spiritual gifts, or if he even suspects you might have a shot at any of this, he's on the move. Why are groups so hard? Because you have an enemy trying to frustrate and shake you.

We wonder why a group may seem divisive or dull. It could be that we have disunity simply because we are sinful human beings, or it could be an intentional spiritual interference being run by the enemy on your community. Likely, it is facing such spiritual interference to some extent. Realize, recognize, and expect the reality of spiritual warfare. Pray and prepare for it. We aren't alone. We have community with God through His Son

Jesus Christ, who has defeated the enemy once for all. We also have the gift of community with one another. We can help one another up when we fall and shield one another so we are not easily affected by the enemy's schemes. That's groups discipleship.

Discerning a spiritual attack is largely being aware of where the enemy is resisting our efforts. Where are the places it's just not working? It feels off? Out of sync? Reminiscent of Babel, we can feel like we're talking to one another but just not understanding. These instances can be the big tip-offs that the enemy is working hard to squash the good God is working in groups, and we need to be both aware and ready.

The enemy doesn't attack what doesn't concern him.

Here's the unexpected encouragement: the enemy doesn't attack what doesn't concern him. If you feel attacked as a group leader in your church, lean into the resistance. There's a reason for it. Maybe the enemy sees potential you don't yet see. Refuse to give the good ground and ask for discernment to see his schemes against the good God has for your group. Go on the offensive.

Here are three ways that can help keep your group from being pelted or pecked to death by the enemy of God.

Prayer Before

A simple yet profound way to prepare for the warfare and the work in group is to pray over the seats in your living room. Many times a prayer team or volunteers will do this before a service meeting on a church campus. We should do the same before our group meets.

Your group members are likely people of habit who sit in the same general spot each time. Use this for the work and warfare. Pray for the individual who sits in each seat by name. Ask for the Lord to give you Scripture to pray for them, pray what you know, what they've shared, ask for God to meet them tonight in group.

Prayer over One Another

The enemy hates friendship and any healthy relationships between Christians. No wonder groups are so hard. The enemy's assault on relationships is constant. So, too, should be our prayers over and for one another.

Spend the first part of group time acknowledging the truth of the warfare in your group. This could be a place to practice confession, either a time of silent confession to God or perhaps even to one another. Pray over and for one another. We've found the best method for this is to pray the "one another" commands of Scripture when you meet (review them in chapter 1). When you are apart, keep praying for one another and what the Lord is doing in your group.

Prayer Afterward

Groups discipleship is spiritual work and warfare. Pray to close the group and include a blessing over the house where it's held. Ask the Lord to guard and guide the souls in the groups and the homes represented. Such prayers are simple but essential to being sober minded and vigilant (1 Pet. 5:8).

When it comes to demons and darkness and the spiritual realm, we face two common dangers in regard to our groups. On one hand, some group members may think we can attribute every problem to demons and spiritual darkness, attempting to ascribe illnesses, injuries, depression, divorces, broken traffic lights, and more to the work of the enemy. But that's not true and gives the enemy way too much credit. Sometimes a cough is a cough, and sometimes a talkative group member is just a talkative group member.

On the other hand, we don't want to attribute nothing to demons and darkness and ignore the possibility. There is a spiritual realm, demons, and a real enemy in our world. We will face the enemy's head-on resistance in our efforts to lead people into community with God and one another. Prepare as leaders and as a community for this reality through prayer. It makes all the difference.

Discuss

1. Have you seen spiritual warfare damage groups you've been part of?

2. What do people tend to overlook about spiritual warfare?

3. In your experience as a member and/or leader, do people tend to overplay or downplay the role of demons and the spiritual world? What is the result?

GROUPS AND HOSPITALITY

"*Divine* hospitality results in *human* hospitality, love, and friendship with and for one another."[4] Jesus said it like this: to "love God and love people" (see Mark 12:30–31) is the greatest commandment. The only way we are capable of love at all is because God "first loved us" (John 4:19). We mimic the Father by showing hospitality to the stranger because we, first, were strangers welcomed into His family.

We mimic the Father by showing hospitality to the stranger because we, first, were strangers welcomed into His family.

It's hard to overstate the importance and prominence of hospitality in the Scriptures. Hospitality is one of the most practical outworkings of God's Spirit as we partner with God to redeem time and relationships as we meet. Most of Jesus's ministry was setting right what had been made wrong in His society. He served the outcast and the foreigner. His focus was the "least of these," inviting them into a new reality, a new family.

If you have eyes to see it, hospitality is *the* thing the New Testament points to as the working out of our faith. "For judgment is without mercy to one who has shown no mercy. Mercy triumphs over judgment. What good is it, my brothers, if someone says he has faith but does not have works? Can that faith save him? If a brother or sister is poorly clothed and lacking in daily food, and one of you says to them, 'Go in peace, be warmed and filled,' without giving them the things needed for the body, what good is that? So also faith by itself, if it does not have works, is dead" (James 2:13–17). We have a tendency to judge the outsider, not show mercy. And without mercy, according to James, our faith is dead.

Or as Jesus says,

> "When the Son of Man comes in his glory, and all the angels with him, then he will sit on his glorious throne. Before him will be gathered all the nations, and he will separate people one from another as a shepherd separates the sheep from the goats. And he will place the sheep on his right, but the goats on the left. Then the King will say to those on his right, 'Come, you who are blessed by my Father, inherit the kingdom prepared for you from the foundation of the world. For I was hungry and you gave me food, I was thirsty and you gave me drink, I was a stranger and you welcomed me, I was naked and you clothed me, I was sick and you visited me, I was in prison and you came to me.' Then the righteous will answer him, saying, 'Lord, when did we see you hungry and feed you, or thirsty and give you drink? And when did we see you as a stranger and welcome

you, or naked and clothe you? And when did we see you sick or in prison and visit you?' And the King will answer them, 'Truly, I say to you, as you did it to one of the least of these my brothers, you did it to me.'

"Then he will say to those on his left, 'Depart from me, you cursed, into the eternal fire prepared for the devil and his angels. For I was hungry and you gave me no food, I was thirsty and you gave me no drink, I was a stranger and you did not welcome me, naked and you did not clothe me, sick and in prison and you did not visit me.' Then they also will answer, saying, 'Lord, when did we see you hungry or thirsty or a stranger or naked or sick or in prison, and did not minister to you?' Then he will answer them, saying, 'Truly, I say to you, as you did not do it to one of the least of these, you did not do it to me.' And these will go away into eternal punishment, but the righteous into eternal life." (Matt. 25:31–46)

Who is cursed? The one who didn't share, clothe, visit, or meet the needs of the least of these. Who is righteous? The one who did. Now, hear us plainly: this is not to undermine the importance of surrendering to Jesus as your Savior in faith. It's the most important step. But it *is* to recognize that faith moves and works. Our faith is worked out in caring for the "least of these," showing you are indeed following Jesus and obeying His command to "love your neighbor as yourself" (Matt. 22:39).

This is what Henri Nouwen says about our culture: "Our society seems to be increasingly full of fearful, defensive, aggressive people anxiously clinging to their property and inclined to look at their surrounding world with suspicion, always expecting an enemy to suddenly appear, intrude and do harm. But still—that is our vocation: to convert the enemy into a guest and to create the free and fearless space where brotherhood and sisterhood can be formed and fully experienced."[5] We invite friends to the table because we have been invited while we were yet enemies of God.

All we've talked through so far focuses on the *why* of hospitality. But what does it practically look like to partner with Jesus in making all things new in our world? We could fill books upon books with the practical outworkings of hospitality.[6] Below are are a few ideas.

Practical Steps

Food. Ministry happens around meals. There is something disarming and inviting about sharing a meal with another person. Make too much of your favorite dish and invite others over.

Passions. What do you enjoy doing? Do it with others, and use it as a vehicle to build relationships for the sake of the gospel.

Least of These. Who are the "least of these" in your context? What does it look like to move toward the margins and let those on the margins step into your space? It can and should change your rhythms, calendar, and preferences, as well as your group.

Don't Do It Alone. This is the beauty of community. You don't have to do it alone. What are you passionate about? What are others in your group passionate about? What would it look like for you and your community to partner with God in bringing about wholeness in your context?

This could be as simple as getting a community soccer game together or hosting a block party. Anything that allows you to interact with those who don't know Jesus.

Acts 2:42–47 is the classic "small groups passage." It's an ideal that rarely gets played out in the modern church. Hospitality gets us closer to that ideal. Read the passage below afresh through the lens of *hospitality*.

> And they devoted themselves to the apostles'
> teaching and the fellowship, to the breaking
> of bread and the prayers. And awe came upon
> every soul, and many wonders and signs were
> being done through the apostles. And all who

believed were together and had all things in common. And they were selling their possessions and belongings and distributing the proceeds to all, as any had need. And day by day, attending the temple together and breaking bread in their homes, they received their food with glad and generous hearts, praising God and having favor with all the people. And the Lord added to their number day by day those who were being saved.

We can't be hospitable if we are a divided and divisive people. The work of hospitality first starts with you. Humanizing those who disagree with you means moving toward them. It's hard to dismiss and dehumanize those you know relationally.

Discuss

1. What polarizing issues do you tend to get upset about? What about the people in your group?

2. Do you regularly fight just to be right? Do arguments break out about issues?

3. How can you lead your group to see other people as humans created in God's image rather than impersonal forces in the culture wars?

CHAPTER 8

Gospel Out

AS SHEPHERDS OF THE local church, our heart yearns for more men and women to experience the life transformation of following Jesus and the freedom He provides, but how do we go about helping others experience this transformation?

GROUPS AND EVANGELISM

Our great concern is that, like Martha in Luke 10, we will do *for* Jesus without being *with* Jesus. The emphasis needs to be on God doing the work. Our role is to partner with Him in that work.

We find it fascinating that Paul, in his letters to churches, actually encourages them to go out and tell everyone about Jesus very few times. We have to ask why.

As Jesus shared the good news, He often taught in parables and questions. He didn't always speak as plainly as people wanted, and He didn't perform miracles every time there was a need. While this could have shouted the truth of His message, He preferred methods that caused people to think deeply and to lean in to know more. Could it be that we, in the church, have assumed some things about evangelism that Jesus didn't assume? At the very least we need to ask this question: Are we evangelizing like Jesus evangelized, or are we doing something different? And if we are doing something different, are we right to do it?

To be clear, we are not saying we shouldn't share our faith. Sharing our faith with those around us is an important aspect of joining Jesus on His mission of making all things new, but what we *are* saying is maybe we should shift our understanding of a "missional mindset." Many in the church have felt deep guilt and shame for not "sharing their faith" with everyone they know and missing the mark for what they expect that is supposed to look like. Maybe they believe they should be shouting the gospel from the street corners or every conversation with an unbelieving friend should end in a gospel presentation.

In Ephesians 4, Paul says the church has been given "apostles, prophets, evangelists, shepherds, and teachers" (see v. 11). One fifth of the leadership roles of the church is evangelist. Praise God for His emphasis and provision for those who have that gift. We should learn from these men and women. Now, not having this gift doesn't mean we should never engage in evangelism; it simply means that our evangelism should be shaped by our gifts.

For example, if someone has the gift of mercy, that should shape the way they go about evangelism. They may serve at a soup kitchen showing mercy to those who have fallen on hard times, and the hope found in Christ will naturally flow from their service, opening up opportunities to discuss the foundation for their love and joy in serving. Just as in gospel hospitality, God welcomed us. We are them and they are us.

Evangelism work is story work. Many don't know how to share about Jesus to others because they don't know themselves and the freedom Christ has unleashed in them. Reflection allows believers in Jesus to understand why they are the way they are and share with others how Jesus has changed their life. Our history becomes his-story. I know—cheezy, right? But it's true. One such story is Clayton's:

> *One night a few years ago a cousin shared the gospel with Clayton, then mailed him "the big ESV Study Bible" and suggested he start reading in the book of John. Clayton read the entire Gospel of John and came to faith. Clayton said he attended a Christmas Eve service at the church. "All of a sudden [in the middle of that service], I was like, uh-oh, I really believe this." He then connected to a small group at the church. "Even after I became a Christian, I was carrying all these old behavior patterns that I wasn't aware of from my old life that I didn't even really know were sinful.*

The guys in my group came along beside me and started sharing with me and challenging me, saying this is what it says in God's Word. When the feelings of guilt or shame come, I remember Jesus." The group was right there when Clayton needed them.

"A group is like a greenhouse to nurture new believers as well as seasoned ones. God is evangelizing the world. When Clayton said yes to Jesus, the group was ready for him."
—Group Leader Testimony

We believe it is better to spend time and energy helping followers of Jesus learn to ask and listen to the Holy Spirit and *then* obey Him. The focus and understanding should shift from "It's *your* job to evangelize the world!" to "*God* is evangelizing His world," and many times He uses us to accomplish that task. This may sound odd compared to Western ideas of evangelism, but all around the world God is leading the charge in miracles that further the gospel, as researched and documented in Craig Keener's *Miracles Today.*[1] Jesus is showing up in dreams of people who have never heard His name.[2] It is our role to partner with God in the renewal of all things. We have to be available. The group has to be available, just like Clayton's cousin was available. Just like Clayton's group was available. We wonder if this is part of what Jesus meant when He said, "My yoke is easy, and my burden is light" (Matt. 11:30). Marc Sayers says it this way: "To partner with God as he brings renewal in the world, in the systems and organizations where we live and lead, we must learn to detect His voice before moving forward; this is a countercultural act in an anxious system, which demands instant action, quick fixes, and fast acting remedies for pain. Waiting on the Lord, seeking His voice, is an act of revolutionary stillness."[3] Below are some practical ideas for developing a love for telling the story of Jesus and sharing with others in your group.

Practical Steps

Big Blue. Using a large piece of poster board (we normally use blue), ask members of your group to write down who they are developing relationships with and praying that God would bring to Himself. Spend some time praying as a group for the names, and bring the poster board back each week for continued prayer and added names. This creates accountability and presence of mind to ask God to redeem those in the sphere of influence of the members of your group. This could be every week for a season or once a month depending on the rhythm of the group.

Fifteen-Second Testimony. The fifteen-second testimony is a beautiful exercise to help men and women learn their own story while inviting others into a conversation about spirituality. Similar to Jesus, this is a way to invite others into a deeper understanding of life and what it means to follow Him. This can be practiced in any space (front-yard barbecue, block party, kids' baseball team, third place, or anywhere natural relationships form in your everyday life). Practice telling what Jesus has done for you specifically in a fifteen-second blurb until everyone is comfortable and ready to share it with others.

Evangelism isn't just about your story, but it's also about the story of redemption for those who are in your community. Evangelism work is group work. One person may use their gift of hospitality to bring a friend to the group and help them feel comfortable, but it may actually be someone else from the group who uses their gift of teaching to help answer their questions about faith. And a different member of the group may use their gift of mercy to help draw out hurts and seek to provide a healing medicine in the good news about the kindness of the Lord.

Does it always happen this cleanly? Of course not, but you get the picture. Evangelism doesn't have to be an individualized activity.

Words and Action. As we mentioned earlier, Jesus spent His time with the "least of these" (Matt. 25:40). He said, "It is not those who are healthy who need a doctor, but those who are sick" (Luke 5:31 csb). Jesus moved toward the marginalized. There seems to be a movement in the upcoming generation that connects a passion and love of Jesus with His justice in the world, and we'd do well to follow suit. Evangelism is both words we say and actions we do.

In his book *Dominion*,[4] Tom Holland, though not a believer in Jesus himself, argues that much of the secular culture today has been shaped by Christianity without even knowing it. Hospitals and caring for the needy and downcast were all part of the Christian ethic. Caring for the least of these is the marker of the early historical church (hospitals, orphanages, women's equality, and more) and a key way the gospel went forward.

At our church we have amazing men and women who care for others and share the gospel. The spiritual fruit they exhibit is something to marvel at. We have learned much from them, and it's a joy to see them use their gifts to build up the body and to expand God's kingdom. We pray the same for you.

Discuss

1. What does it look like in your context to reach back to our historic faith and bring about the renewal of all things in your community?

2. Are any of these evangelism ideas new or challenging to you?

3. Is there a person with the gift of evangelism in your group who can help you grow in this area?

Those Who Go

Some of us are better at goodbyes than others. Some are quick to say goodbye. Rip off the bandage. Fare thee well. That's life. Others say goodbye several times, intended or not. Like saying "good night" before you both realize you're actually headed toward the same elevator, this may or may not be a gift of anything but awkwardness.

Then there's the couched-in-familiarity, "see ya later" final greeting, both of you pausing for a moment after you say it, realizing that, well, you probably won't. We are all somewhat clumsy with our farewells. Probably because they reintroduce us all over again to the fact that we are not in ultimate control of our lives or anyone else's. Yet saying goodbye is the way of the sending church.

In my own heart, I'm (Jared) prone to want to keep my community to myself and not share them, but the book of Acts presses me on this preference. In it I always find a repeating pattern: as Christ is building His church, He brings His people together in groups for a time, for seasons, and to accomplish kingdom work. Some stay together to nurture the work. Others are called out to start other works.

Two thousand years later, this is still the ebb and flow of a healthy Christian community. Godly people hold one another with an open hand, knowing God might call them to new work at any time. The patterns God showed me in Acts caused me to reconsider the Great Commission of Christ in Matthew 28. By His Word, He gently began to pry my tightly closed fist open, with me screaming all the way, "These are my friends, God. This is who I need with me to follow You. They speak into my life. We've been through a lot together. I'm not letting them go."

In His grace to me, He began leading many of the people I held most dear in this way out of my proximity. This continues today for me, and I guess it's the same for you. He still leads friends away to other kingdom works, but He's growing me to be quicker to say, "O God, these brothers and sisters don't belong to me. I'm not the master of their days; Jesus is."

Even in the community of my own family—my wife and my son—I must recognize Jesus commands their destinies. "God, they are not mine to do with and to direct as I please. Under Your leadership I will lead them, but Lord, You have Your way with them."

The truth is, godly people must hold one another with an open hand. Godly people who are about the gospel say goodbye often, confident in our union together as the family of God and confident that we will celebrate again. We *will* see one another again at the marriage supper of the Lamb. We will be with God together. For all time.

But now, just for a little while, we have little time to waste. Jesus's commands override any attempts to build our own little castle of community to rule over. God is so much greater. We're called to hold one another with an open hand. This is the legacy of disciple-making into which the first disciples were called—a call that still resounds.

It still resounds.

We are part of an ages-old, ongoing, epic work of the Creator God, whose image we bear and who is transforming us still by His work in Christ through our Christian community. It says something about who we are as the body of Christ that we have said many gospel goodbyes. Christians living rightly consistently say goodbye.

No one in our lives is with us constantly, save for the Lord Jesus by His Holy Spirit. In this we trust as we say our goodbyes with great hope.

Discuss

1. Do you struggle to say goodbye more than you struggle to say hello, or is it the other way around?

2. How will you prepare your group for when you leave to start another group? Who will you prepare to take your place?

Those Who Stay Behind

It's a fact of the faithful life that gospel people say goodbye. Some leave the familiar for the unknown as the Lord leads, but not all of us are headed for the ends of the earth.

Some of us are right where we are supposed to be, and we're going to be here awhile. That may thrill you or fill you with discouragement, but take heart and know that some believers aren't called away to be the tip of the gospel spear. Some of us are called to stay together and stay behind to nurture the work.

This is the template of the book of Acts, just as we discovered earlier. The people of God are brought together for a time, in a place, to accomplish a work beyond any of their individual capabilities—world-changing stuff. Then some of them are led away to the next adventure. Others stay behind to cultivate the local Christian community in the quietly unfolding epic of the day-to-day.

Charles Haddon Spurgeon speaks of this legitimate necessity that some stay behind: "Fiery spirits may dash forward over untrodden paths to learn fresh truth, and win more souls to Jesus; but some of a more conservative spirit may be well engaged in reminding the church of her ancient faith, and restoring her fainting sons. Every position has its duties."[5]

Staying Behind Is Dangerous. After the car pulls away or the plane departs, we walk back into our familiar surroundings and fight the feeling that we're stuck. The departure of friends makes us sad; we are happy and prayerful for them, of course, but they will be missed. It won't be the same as it was. Know the inherent dangers of staying behind. It's far too easy to get nostalgic about our world as it once was and fail to acknowledge all that God is doing in the world now.

Also, watch for the seed of envious defeat. It feels like the brothers and sisters who left are making more important decisions and facing greater challenges in their lives. We consider our choices, what led us here, and we reflect. We must guard against an unhealthy introspection that inhibits our ability to take action on the home front.

This is the danger of staying behind. We won't endure a frontal assault, but we will sometimes feel as though our position is surrounded. Like David in Psalm 55, we may long to sprout wings and fly away from what are often personal attacks. These aren't some distant native peoples rejecting us; they're often friends. In this, staying requires a special brand of courage to aid, over the course of time, the doubting, desponding, wavering, joyless souls of others—and a Holy Spirit-aided bravery to fight our own unhealthy introspection in the middle of it all.

Staying Behind Is Crucial. What do we do if we stay behind? We learn to say goodbye in a different way: an active way, a joyful way.

We consider why we are where we are. We ask God to inform and superintend the mission He has for us in this place, being ever mindful that we, too, are a crucial part of the coming of Christ's kingdom.

Has God called you to stay behind? Be faithful in the so-called mundane (as if there were such a thing in the life of a child of God!). Challenge yourself in your daily schedule. Pray for the Lord to bring a friend whom you can mentor/disciple into your path. Ask for friendships with people who don't think, look, or believe as you do. Dig in with them. Show them the reality of the community of God's people. Cultivate it in your church and small group as you would a garden season after season. Invest deeply in your local church. Lean into the lean years, and let them be anything but ho-hum.

Challenge yourself to get out. Visit gospel-preaching churches and church plants and see how the Lord is moving in your city, state, and country.

Take charge of the common grace of modern communication and support those who have gone. Encourage your friends who have left for uncharted waters. Write them. FaceTime, Zoom, or Skype with them. Get the word out to others in your community about the work your friends are doing. Use it as an opportunity to talk of God's gospel going forth and how others may join in. Support them with your prayers; support them with your resources. Show hospitality to them when they return for a visit. Do not grow weary of doing good on their behalf. Let it be said of those who stayed behind that we contended for the gospel with the same zeal, with the same kingdom mindset, with the same faithfulness as those who said goodbye.

After all, we are all walking toward the same eternal destination. We will all be together again with some great stories to tell. And we will have all of eternity to listen and be together with God and one another.

Discuss

1. How can you prepare those who stay behind (including yourself) for the void left by those who go?

2. How is it different when people leave for good reasons (planting a new group or moving to a better life situation) than when they leave for bad reasons (hurt or walking away from the faith)?

3. What are some ways to celebrate good departures and mourn hard ones?

4. How can you include going and staying in the regular prayer life of your group?

Groups Now More than Ever

"All over the world, and for decades, people have been embracing their interior lives more and interacting less, and they are doing this by choice."[1]

NO REMINDER LIKE THE present times that the art of leading a community is hard. Just *being in* a community takes work. And it's a discipline that is verifiably declining. That's why we are writing. We want to recapture your love of groups ministry. Or fan it into flame for the first time.

Groups are an ancient art form charged to the church through more than fifty commands for our relationships to one another. Before eternity arrives and the believers are all together at God's table with all the time in the universe to tell stories of what He's done, we have this work to do. We are still in the story!

Like authors at the midway point of the novel, we've got some challenges before we finish our part.

GROUPS ARE GARDENS

Eugene Peterson said,

> The person . . . who looks for quick results in the seed planting of well-doing will be disappointed. If I want potatoes for dinner tomorrow, it will do me little good to go out and plant potatoes in my garden tonight. There are long stretches of darkness and invisibility and silence that separate planting and reaping. During the stretches of waiting there is cultivating and weeding and nurturing and planting still other seeds.[2]

In this vein of faith, do we fast and pray for friendships that may not be there . . . yet? Are we an authentic person worthy of being a friend? Are we who we say we are? Cultivation of relationships of trust requires authenticity of character as well as availability and investment. You can't complain that no one has time for you if you don't have time for them either. Is there room in your schedule for a deep friend or two? Or rather, is there time to begin cultivating what it takes to grow such a friendship? Both parties have to be committed. That's relational accountability. You do what you say you're going to do. You don't flake out.

Gardening is an art form, too. The soil must be worked. The holes must be dug. The seeds must be planted and watered. Ultimately, though, there's nothing we can do to force growth. It is a work of God. He's the one who breaks open the seed and brings forth life, and He's doing the same work of cultivation in our groups, both individually and corporately. We bring the right elements together and ask God to work, and then we wait. We wait on Him to do what He has done in the past and what we know He will do in the future. He is faithful to bring the fruit.

We till the soil and prepare the space with the spiritual practices we see in the Bible: the Word, prayer, food, fellowship, encouragement, accountability, and sharing faith, and then we trust God to break open the little tomb-like seeds and sprout forth in our life and the lives of those in our group. We place the extra chairs out and pray over each chair that represents a soul who will sit with others to celebrate the truth that the Father sent the Son. We raise empty hands of faith and ask the Lord to fill us with great fruit that serves those around us. This is God's garden, His group, and He will cultivate what He pleases.

Neither gardens nor groups grow overnight. There's the work of going after the already existing existential weeds. Are people even able to seed (much less grow) relationships of trust anymore? Many of us have lost fortitude in friendships; someone does something we don't like, we don't stick it out. We easily dispose them and say, "Well, we were friends then. But I'm going to go find some others who agree with me more often." It's easy to see why too many of us give up. The garden of trust is too overtaken with weeds and hazards.

One way to work the garden and keep it is to *keep at it*. The routines of group life and community in your local church are key: "Simply being around other people has benefits," writes Jeffrey Hall. "Classic studies of the power of proximity show how just living near people increases the chances of friendship. Such familiarity lowers individuals' perceptions of risk and increases our effort toward interacting in more responsive and attentive ways toward one another."[3]

One another. *Groups exist for community with God and one another.* We need one another as the society shifts toward interiority and less effort to care for one another. This is Acts 2 stuff. People are not the barrier to self-preservation and fulfillment. *The people in your group are a partial inheritance from the Lord right now.* Are you grateful for the inheritance God has given you in this group? If you had to chart out how much you pray for your group and group members versus how often you complain about them, what would that chart look like? Might that be the problem? Might it also point to a transformational solution?

Practicing the art of community, the "one anothers" of Scripture, and (not so) simply showing up expectant for God to move every week is powerful. Routines begin the gardens where relationships grow. That includes your relationship with God. God is also in your group each week. He wants to do work. He likes meeting with your group. Such regularly shared belief, talking, and taking care of one another in a group softens our hardened hearts, reduces our need to be right, increases our desire to be righteous, and helps us become more focused on others than self.

It also gives us greater fortitude for the church and for friendships—which, if we are all honest, is what we want. We are made by God for fellowship with Him and one another. But that's painstaking art, not lab science.

Think about the threats facing Ruth and Naomi. Jonathan and David. Jesus and His disciples. Barnabas and Paul. They developed intense and godly relationships of trust under trying circumstances. That's a key: friendships are often formed in the crucible of faith. God was doing a work in them. And they shared it with one another. Maybe that's the start for the group.

What is the work God is doing in you? Do you see Him working in someone else in your group? God is working to cultivate growth from the moments spent in community. We join Him in the work, tilling the soil, planting the seeds, and reaping the harvest when we walk faithfully with Him, led by Him as the ultimate Gardener who also prunes and cares for those He loves.

So goes groups, so goes the church.
So goes the church, so goes groups.

Notes

Chapter 1: Why Groups?

1. Francis A. Schaeffer, *The Mark of the Christian* (Downers Grove, IL: IVP Books, 2006), 59.

2. Martin Luther, "Preface to the German Mass and Order of Service," *Luther Works*, vol. 53, Helmut T. Lehman, ed. (Minneapolis: Fortress Press, 1965), 63–64.

3. Joel Comiskey, *2000 Years of Small Groups: A History of Cell Ministry in the Church* (Lima, OH: CCS Publishing, 2014), 81.

Chapter 2: Home Base for Transformation

1. Ephesians 2:19; Matthew 12:46–50.

2. Ephesians 4:16; 1 Corinthians 12:26–27; Romans 12:5; Colossians 1:18; Colossians 3:14–16; Ephesians 1:20–23.

3. Joseph H. Hellerman, *When the Church Was a Family: Recapturing Jesus's Vision for Authentic Christian Community* (Nashville: B&H Academic, 2009), 1.

4. Patricia Armstrong, "Bloom's Taxonomy," Vanderbilt University Center for Teaching, https://cft.vanderbilt.edu/guides-sub-pages/blooms-taxonomy.

5. Todd Wilson, "The Integrated Pastor: Toward an Embodied and Embedded Spiritual Formation," Center for Pastor Theologians, October 22, 2018, https://www.pastortheologians.com/media/2018/12/14/todd-wilson-the-integrated-pastor-toward-an-embodied-and-embedded-spiritual-formation.

6. Jim Wilder and Michel Hendricks, *The Other Half of Church: Christian Community, Brain Science, and Overcoming Spiritual Stagnation* (Chicago: Moody Publishers, 2020), 79.

Chapter 3: Groups as Deep Community

1. Dietrich Bonhoeffer, *Life Together: A Discussion of Christian Fellowship* (San Francisco: HarperSanFrancisco, 1978), 27.

2. "Group Leaders," North Point Ministries, https://groupleaders.org/new-leader-training.

3. Jim Wilder and Michel Hendricks, *The Other Half of Church: Christian Community, Brain Science, and Overcoming Spiritual Stagnation* (Chicago: Moody Publishers, 2020), 21.

4. Bonhoeffer, *Life Together*, 112.

5. Rosaria Champagne Butterfield, *The Gospel Comes with a House Key: Practicing Radically Ordinary Hospitality in Our Post-Christian World* (Wheaton, IL: Crossway, 2018), 111.

6. Butterfield, *The Gospel Comes with a House Key*, 111.

7. Jennie Allen, *Find Your People: Building Deep Community in a Lonely World* (Colorado Springs: WaterBrook, 2022), 52.

Chapter 4: Conflict and Confession

1. Paul Tripp, "How to Fight Right," *Journal of Biblical Counseling*, vol. 27, no. 2 (September 16, 2019), 69–71.

Chapter 5: Groups Begin and End

1. Ryan T. Hartwig, Courtney W. Davis, and Jason A. Sniff, *Leading Small Groups That Thrive: Five Shifts to Take Your Small Group to the Next Level* (Grand Rapids: Zondervan Reflective, 2020), 19.

2. Tod E. Bolsinger, *Canoeing the Mountains: Christian Leadership in Uncharted Territory* (Downers Grove, IL: IVP Books, 2015), 67.

Chapter 6: Groups Gathered

1. Francis A. Schaeffer, *The Complete Works of Francis A. Schaeffer: A Christian Worldview*, vol. 4, A Christian View of the Church (Wheaton, IL: Crossway, 1982).

2. Roger W. Gehring, *House Church and Mission: The Importance of Household Structures in Early Christianity* (Peabody, Massachusetts: Hendrickson Publishers, Inc., 2009).

3. Robert C. Culley, *Oral Tradition and Historicity. In Studies on the Ancient Palestinian World.* Ed. J. W. Wevers and D. B. Redford. Toronto: University of Toronto Press, 1972).

4. "Wesley's Rules for Band-Societies: Drawn up December 25, 1738," Miscellaneous Writings, House Church, https://housechurch.org/miscellaneous/wesley_band-societies.html.

Chapter 7: Groups and Loving One Another Well

1. Jeffrey A. Hall, "The Price We Pay for Being Less Social," *Wall Street Journal*, August 11, 2022.

2. Francis A. Schaeffer, *The Complete Works of Francis Schaeffer: A Christian Worldview*, vol. 3, A Christian View of Spirituality (Wheaton, IL: Crossway, 1982), 281.

3. Sam Storms, *Understanding Spiritual Gifts: A Comprehensive Guide* (Grand Rapids: Zondervan Reflective, 2020), 18.

4. Joshua W. Jipp, Saved by *Faith and Hospitality* (Grand Rapids: William B. Eerdmans, 2017), 54.

5. Henri J. M. Nouwen, *Reaching Out: The Three Movements of the Spiritual Life* (New York: Doubleday, 1975), 65–66.

6. Excellent books are Rosaria Butterfield, *The Gospel Comes with a House Key* (Wheaton, IL: Crossway, 2018), and Jipp, *Saved by Faith and Hospitality*.

Chapter 8: Gospel Out

1. Craig Keener, *Miracles Today* (Grand Rapids: Baker Academic, 2021), 1.

2. Darren Carlson, "When Muslims Dream of Jesus," The Gospel Coalition, May 31, 2018, https://www.thegospelcoalition.org/article/muslims-dream-jesus.

3. Mark Sayers, *A Non-Anxious Presence: How a Changing and Complex World Will Create a Remnant of Renewed Christian Leaders* (Chicago: Moody Publishers, 2022), 162.

4. Tom Holland, *Dominion: How the Christian Revolution Remade the World* (New York: Basic Books, 2019).

5. Charles H. Spurgeon, *Devotional Classics of C. H. Spurgeon* (Gaithersburg, MD: Sovereign Grace Publishers, 2000), 18.

Conclusion: Groups Now More than Ever

1. Jeffrey A. Hall, "The Price We Pay for Being Less Social," *Wall Street Journal*, August 11, 2022, www.wsj.com/articles/price-we-pay-for-being-less-social-11660068416.

2. Eugene H. Peterson, *The Contemplative Pastor: Returning to the Art of Spiritual Direction* (Grand Rapids: William B. Eerdmans, 1993), 3.

3. Hall, "The Price We Pay for Being Less Social."

Also available in this series

WITH OTHERS TO COME

Available where books are sold.

DON'T LEAD COMMUNITY MINISTRY...

ALONE.

COACHING
COLLABORATIVES
CONSULTING

CMMNTY / LDRSHP